boundary between the two is not always easy to draw. Is there any practical difference between a criminal gang which grows narcotics and guards its crop with guns, and insurgents who grow drugs to finance their rebellion? Just where does the boundary lie between an off-duty soldier who sexually assaults someone, and a deliberate military campaign of rape, which can be a war crime?

These two approaches to human security are both people-centered, and are complementary rather than contradictory. But because the "broad" concept includes everything from poverty to genocide, it has so far proved too all-embracing to be helpful in policy development.

This atlas, based on data from the *Human Security Report 2005* (Oxford University Press) and the *Human Security Brief 2006*, uses the *narrow* concept of human security, and maps the incidence and severity of global violence.

It is

Par

War looks at the decline in armed conflicts which involve government forces – both conflicts between states, and conflicts within states.

Part 2: Warlords and Killing Fields examines armed conflicts which do not involve government forces, as well as genocides and other "one-sided" mass killings of civilians.

Part 3: Counting the Dead asks how far we can rely on the reported death tolls, from all forms of armed conflict as well as from one-sided violence.

Part 4: Measuring Human Rights Abuse shows that we have few reliable figures on torture, child soldiers, ethnic cleansing, and other gross human rights violations, but that some comparisons can be made between different states.

Part 5: Causes of War, Causes of Peace explores the reasons why armed conflicts and their death tolls have declined, and still seem to be declining.

Other Titles in the *mini*atlas Series

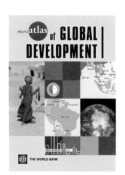

miniAtlas of Global Development
An at-a-glance guide to the most pressing development issues facing the world today. Highlights key social, economic, and environmental data for 208 of the world's economies.

ISBN13: 978-0-8213-5596-1
ISBN10: 0-8213-5596-1

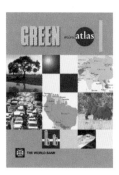

Green miniAtlas
A snapshot, presented in maps and charts, of the world's most urgent environmental challenges: increasing pollution, the rising demand for energy and food, declining biodiversity, and the pressure on water resources.

ISBN13: 978-0-8213-5870-2
ISBN10: 0-8213-5870-7

miniAtlas of Millennium Development Goals: Building a Better World
How far are we towards meeting the Millennium Development Goals? And what resources are needed to help those countries that are not on track? An insightful and practical guide to important contemporary global concerns.

ISBN13: 978-0-8213-6175-7
ISBN10: 0-8213-6175-9

Available at better bookstores
To order go to **www.worldbank.org/publications**
or email: books@worldbank.org

*mini*atlas of HUMAN SECURITY

THE WORLD BANK
Washington, D.C.

Human Security Report Project
Vancouver, Canada

The International Bank for Reconstruction and Development / The World Bank
1818 H Street, NW
Washington, DC 20433
Telephone 202-473-1000
Internet www.worldbank.org
E-mail feedback@worldbank.org

and

Human Security Report Project
School for International Studies
Suite 2400
Simon Fraser University
515 West Hastings Street
Vancouver BC V6B 5K3
Canada
Internet www.hsrgroup.org

ISBN: 978-0-8213-7221-0
E-ISBN: 978-0-8213-7222-7
DOI: 10.1596/978-0-8213-7221-0

Published for the World Bank and the Human Security Report Project by
Myriad Editions
59 Lansdowne Place, Brighton BN3 1FL, UK
www.MyriadEditions.com

Printed and bound in Hong Kong

This work was carried out with the aid of a grant from the International Development Research Centre, Ottawa, Canada.

Additional support was received from the UK Department for International Development.

Editorial consultant: Jon Tinker, Panos Institute of Canada   www.panoscanada.ca

The miniAtlas of Human Security draws on material first published in the Human Security Report 2005: War and Peace in the 21st Century, an Oxford University Press publication. It also draws on the findings of the Human Security Brief 2006.

The Human Security Report Project (HSRP) was based at the Human Security Centre, Liu Institute for Global Issues, University of British Columbia, from February 2002 until May 2007. In May 2007 the HSRP relocated to the School for International Studies, Simon Fraser University.

Contents

Preface

In a world afflicted by major wars, gross human rights abuse, and the threat of ever-more-deadly terrorist attacks, it is not surprising that most people believe political violence to be on the increase.

But, as the *miniAtlas of Human Security* demonstrates, the conventional wisdom is quite wrong. There were 40 percent fewer armed conflicts in 2005 than at the end of the Cold War a decade and a half earlier. The decline in high-casualty conflicts (those with 1,000 or more reported battle-deaths each year) has been even greater – an 80 percent drop over the same period.

The number of refugees has also declined since the end of the Cold War, reflecting the reduction in the political violence that is a major cause of people fleeing their homes. And, although there is little reliable information, it seems likely that the number of children serving as soldiers in rebel and government forces has declined too.

War has aptly been described as "development in reverse." Its consequences include death, injury, increased disease and malnutrition, large-scale destruction of infrastructure and health services, massive capital flight, and loss of investment. According to Paul Collier, the cost of a typical civil war is around $50 billion.

The fact that wars exacerbate poverty is hardly surprising, but the evidence strongly suggests that poverty may also be a driver of war. Low incomes per capita mean weak state capacity and create incentives for impoverished, unemployed, and often desperate youth to join rebel movements.

The maps and graphics in the *miniAtlas of Human Security* reveal the surprising changes in war trends since the end of the Cold War. They also highlight the associations between armed conflicts and economic and political development. The text that accompanies the map spreads provides concise analyses of the issues being reviewed.

Former UN Secretary-General Kofi Annan said that there can be no development without security – and no security without development. The *miniAtlas of Human Security*, created by the team that produces the influential *Human Security Report*, helps explain why.

Timor-Leste

Eskinder
Debebe/
UN Photo

5

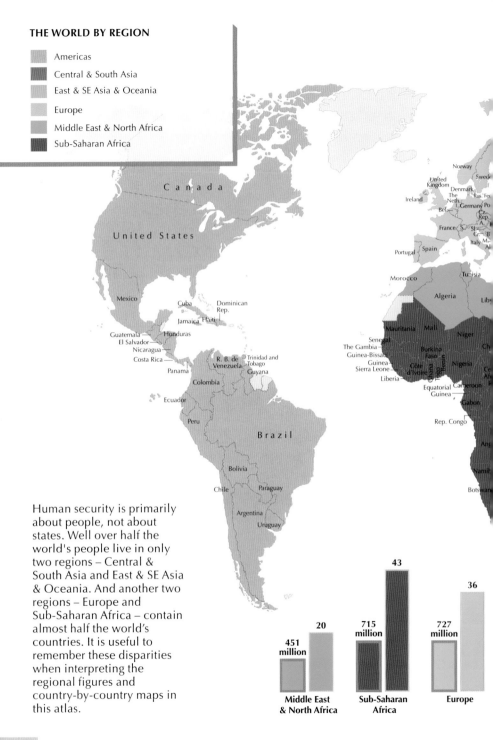

THE WORLD BY REGION

- Americas
- Central & South Asia
- East & SE Asia & Oceania
- Europe
- Middle East & North Africa
- Sub-Saharan Africa

Canada

United States

Norway
Sweden
United Kingdom
Denmark
Ireland
The Neth.
Bel.
Germany
Po
Cz. Rep.
A.
France
S.
Sl.
Cr.
B
Italy
M.
Al.
Portugal
Spain
Tunisia
Morocco
Algeria
Lib

Mexico
Cuba
Dominican Rep.
Jamaica Haiti
Guatemala
El Salvador
Honduras
Nicaragua
Costa Rica
Panama
Colombia
Ecuador
Peru

R. B. de Venezuela
Trinidad and Tobago
Guyana

Mauritania
Mali
Niger
Ch
Senegal
The Gambia
Guinea-Bissau
Guinea
Sierra Leone
Liberia
Burkina Faso
Côte d'Ivoire
Ghana
Togo
Benin
Nigeria
Ce
Af
Equatorial Guinea
Cameroon
Gabon
Rep. Congo

Brazil

Bolivia
Chile
Paraguay
Argentina
Uruguay

Ang
Namib.
Botswa

Human security is primarily about people, not about states. Well over half the world's people live in only two regions – Central & South Asia and East & SE Asia & Oceania. And another two regions – Europe and Sub-Saharan Africa – contain almost half the world's countries. It is useful to remember these disparities when interpreting the regional figures and country-by-country maps in this atlas.

Middle East & North Africa — 451 million, 20

Sub-Saharan Africa — 715 million, 43

Europe — 727 million, 36

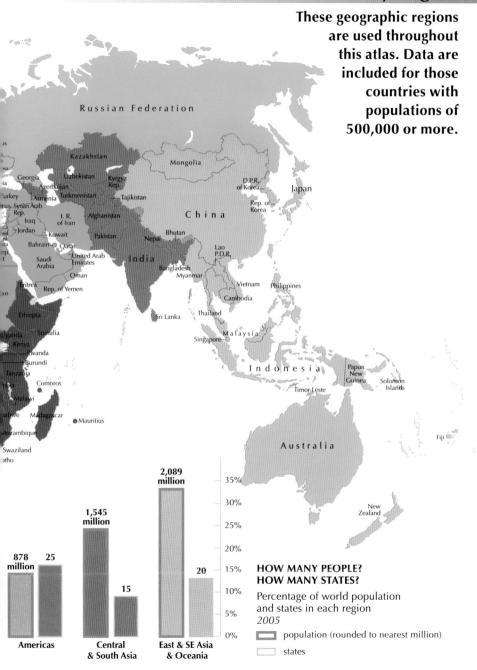

The World by Region

These geographic regions are used throughout this atlas. Data are included for those countries with populations of 500,000 or more.

Russian Federation

Kazakhstan

Mongolia

D.P.R.
of Korea

Japan

Georgia
Uzbekistan
Kyrgyz
Rep.

Azerbaijan

Armenia

Turkmenistan

Tajikistan

Rep. of
Korea

Turkey
Syrian Arab
Rep.

Iraq

I. R.
of Iran

Afghanistan

China

Jordan
Kuwait

Bahrain
Qatar

Pakistan

Bhutan

Nepal

Lao
P.D.R.

Saudi
Arabia

United Arab
Emirates

India

Oman

Bangladesh

Myanmar

Eritrea
Rep. of Yemen

Vietnam

Philippines

Cambodia

Ethiopia

Sri Lanka

Thailand

Uganda
Somalia

Kenya

Malaysia

Singapore

Rwanda

Burundi

Tanzania

Comoros

Indonesia

Papua
New
Guinea

Solomon
Islands

Malawi

Timor-Leste

Madagascar

Mauritius

Mozambique

Australia

Fiji

Swaziland

New
Zealand

2,089 million

1,545 million

878 million **25**

15

20

35%
30%
25%
20%
15%
10%
5%
0%

Americas

Central & South Asia

East & SE Asia & Oceania

HOW MANY PEOPLE?
HOW MANY STATES?

Percentage of world population and states in each region
2005

population (rounded to nearest million)

states

When States Go to War

Since the end of the Cold War, armed conflicts around the world have declined substantially.

The world is becoming less war-prone. The number of civil wars dropped by three-quarters from 1992 to 2005. And the number of international conflicts has been falling since the mid-1970s – the most sustained decline in two centuries.

The 1945 United Nations Charter promised "to save succeeding generations from the scourge of war." Today, the UN collects statistics on everything from schools and hunger to measles and coal mines. But on war, it has no official figures. Why not?

The short answer is politics. In 2005, all armed conflicts were being fought within states, not between them. Many governments believe that internal violence is a domestic matter, and no business of the UN. So they will not provide details.

Existing global statistics on wars, conflicts and genocides come from a handful of research institutes. Each uses different methods, and few update their figures annually. This atlas draws on data from the *Human Security Report 2005* and the *Human Security Brief 2006*.

The main types of armed conflict are described overleaf. Some individual conflicts are a hybrid of different types of violence. The 2003 US-led invasion of Iraq, for example, started as an inter-state conflict but soon became an internationalized intra-state conflict. Iraq also suffers from non-state conflicts between sectarian militias.

Worldwide, the number of state-based conflicts increased steadily from the early 1950s until the end of the Cold War. 1992 marks the beginning of a sharp decline. But this trend was not the same across all regions. On the one hand, the Cold War had frozen many tensions, which in some regions exploded into violence. And on the other hand, the post-Cold War era reduced superpower sponsorship of civil wars and allowed a surge of international peacemaking. These various causes of war and peace are explored in the final section of the atlas.

Overall, the trends in state-based conflicts are remarkably encouraging. The next section of this atlas examines the two other main forms of organized political violence: non-state conflicts and one-sided violence.

Israel/
Gaza Strip
Ahikam Seri /
Panos Pictures

Definitions

Wars are high-intensity armed conflicts. Whether a conflict qualifies as a war depends on the number of battle-deaths that occur in a year.

Battle-deaths include civilians caught in the crossfire as well as combatants, but not deaths from war-induced disease and starvation, nor the deliberate killing of unarmed civilians.

An *armed conflict* with over 1,000 battle-deaths in a year is called a *war*. When the number of battle-deaths in an armed conflict falls below 25 per year, it is no longer counted as a conflict.

There are two main types of *armed conflict*. This section of the atlas covers *state-based conflicts:* those that involve at least one national government. *Non-state conflicts*, fought between militias, warlords, or ethnic groups, without the involvement of the national government, are covered in the next section.

There are four forms of state-based conflict (called *wars* if they cause more than 1,000 battle-deaths a year):

- **Inter-state conflicts** are between states. Few in number, these have declined unevenly since the late 1980s.
- **Extra-state conflicts** are between a state and an armed group outside the state's own territory. These are mostly colonial conflicts.
- **Intra-state conflicts** (which include civil wars) are between a government and a non-state group. In 1946, 47% of conflicts were intra-state. By 2005, the figure was 100%.
- **Internationalized intra-state conflicts** occur when the government, or an armed group opposing it, receives military support from one or more foreign states, as in Afghanistan since 2001.

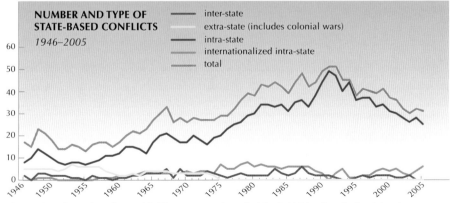

The number of armed conflicts trebled from 1946 to the end of the Cold War, then declined sharply.

REGIONAL DISTRIBUTION OF STATE-BASED CONFLICTS
2005

- Americas
- Central & South Asia
- East & SE Asia & Oceania
- Europe
- Middle East & North Africa
- Sub-Saharan Africa

Total: 31

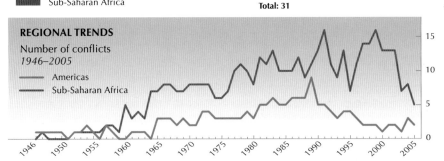

REGIONAL TRENDS
Number of conflicts
1946–2005

- Americas
- Sub-Saharan Africa

Americas: Armed conflicts, driven in part by Cold War politics, increased from the 1960s to the end of the 1980s, especially in Central America, and then fell significantly.

Sub-Saharan Africa: Conflicts rose unevenly during the post-colonial period from the mid-1960s to the end of the century, but have been falling since 1999.

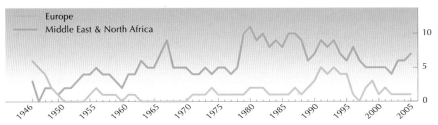

- Europe
- Middle East & North Africa

Europe: The Cold War was associated with four decades of uneasy peace from the 1950s until the end of the 1980s. Violence in the Balkans followed the breakup of the Soviet Union and Yugoslavia in the 1990s.

Middle East & North Africa: Armed conflicts increased unevenly from the 1940s to 1980, but with growing political repression they have since declined by nearly 40%.

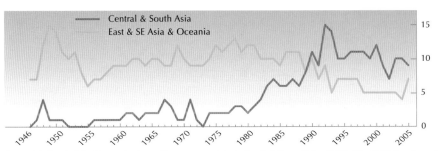

- Central & South Asia
- East & SE Asia & Oceania

Central & South Asia: The region's conflicts were mainly in South Asia until the 1970s. The 1991 breakup of the Soviet Union triggered fresh conflicts in Central Asia (including the Caucasus).

East & SE Asia & Oceania: Conflicts have dropped by 46% since 1978, a decline associated with rising prosperity, democratization, and the end of large-scale foreign military intervention.

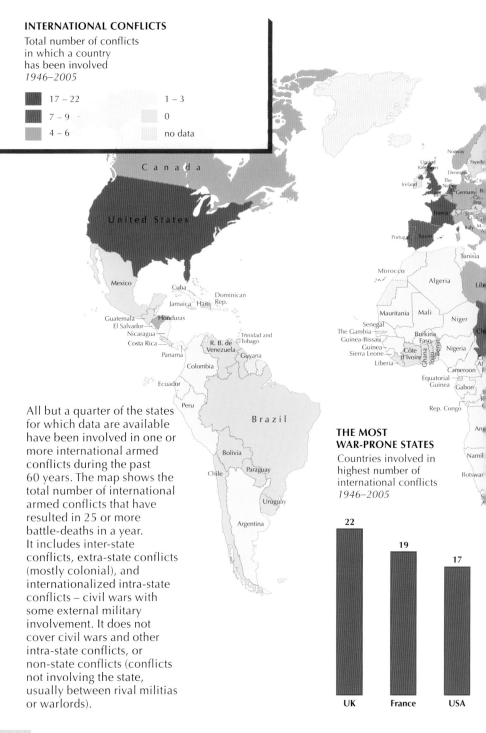

INTERNATIONAL CONFLICTS

Total number of conflicts
in which a country
has been involved
1946–2005

- 17 – 22
- 7 – 9
- 4 – 6
- 1 – 3
- 0
- no data

All but a quarter of the states
for which data are available
have been involved in one or
more international armed
conflicts during the past
60 years. The map shows the
total number of international
armed conflicts that have
resulted in 25 or more
battle-deaths in a year.
It includes inter-state
conflicts, extra-state conflicts
(mostly colonial), and
internationalized intra-state
conflicts – civil wars with
some external military
involvement. It does not
cover civil wars and other
intra-state conflicts, or
non-state conflicts (conflicts
not involving the state,
usually between rival militias
or warlords).

THE MOST WAR-PRONE STATES

Countries involved in
highest number of
international conflicts
1946–2005

UK	France	USA
22	19	17

International Armed Conflicts

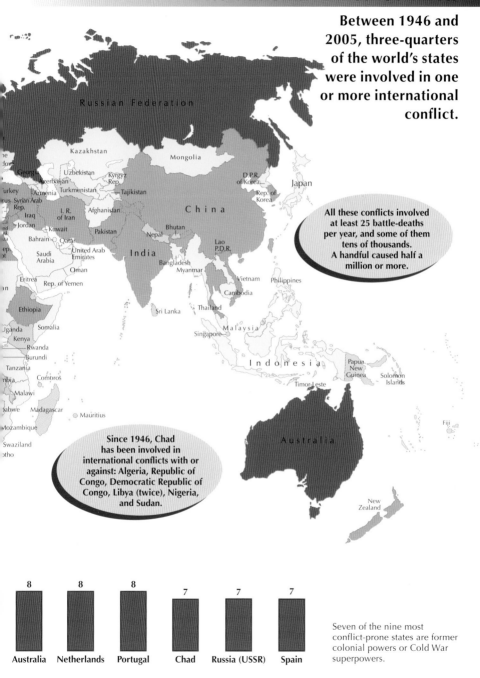

Between 1946 and 2005, three-quarters of the world's states were involved in one or more international conflict.

All these conflicts involved at least 25 battle-deaths per year, and some of them tens of thousands. A handful caused half a million or more.

Since 1946, Chad has been involved in international conflicts with or against: Algeria, Republic of Congo, Democratic Republic of Congo, Libya (twice), Nigeria, and Sudan.

8	8	8	7	7	7
Australia	Netherlands	Portugal	Chad	Russia (USSR)	Spain

Seven of the nine most conflict-prone states are former colonial powers or Cold War superpowers.

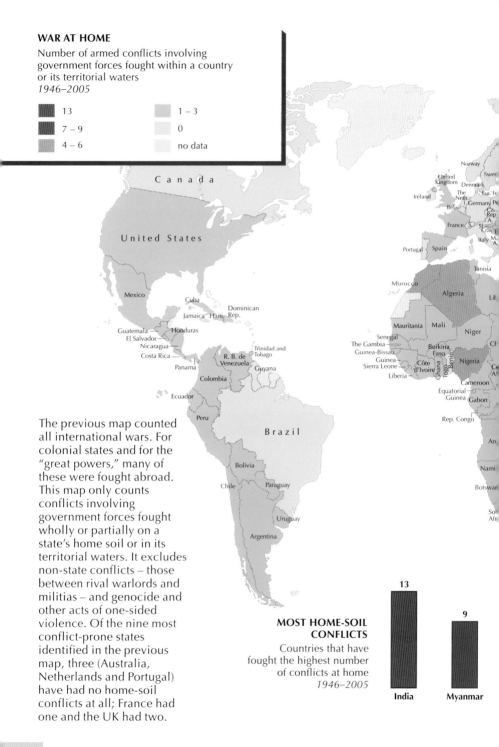

WAR AT HOME

Number of armed conflicts involving government forces fought within a country or its territorial waters
1946–2005

■ 13	■ 1 – 3		
■ 7 – 9	■ 0		
■ 4 – 6	▨ no data		

Canada

United States

Mexico
Cuba
Jamaica Haiti Dominican Rep.
Guatemala
El Salvador
Nicaragua
Costa Rica
Panama
R. B. de Venezuela
Trinidad and Tobago
Guyana
Colombia
Ecuador
Peru
Brazil
Bolivia
Chile Paraguay
Uruguay
Argentina

Norway
United Kingdom Swec
Denmark
Ireland The Neth. Rus. Fe
Bel. Germany Po
Rep.
France Sl
Italy M.
Portugal Spain
Tunisia
Morocco Algeria Lib
Mauritania Mali Niger
Senegal
The Gambia Burkina Faso Ch
Guinea-Bissau Guinea Côte d'Ivoire Nigeria
Sierra Leone Ghana Togo Benin
Liberia
Cameroon
Equatorial Guinea Gabon
Rep. Congo
An
Nami
Botswar
So
Afr

The previous map counted all international wars. For colonial states and for the "great powers," many of these were fought abroad. This map only counts conflicts involving government forces fought wholly or partially on a state's home soil or in its territorial waters. It excludes non-state conflicts – those between rival warlords and militias – and genocide and other acts of one-sided violence. Of the nine most conflict-prone states identified in the previous map, three (Australia, Netherlands and Portugal) have had no home-soil conflicts at all; France had one and the UK had two.

MOST HOME-SOIL CONFLICTS

Countries that have fought the highest number of conflicts at home
1946–2005

13	9
India	Myanmar

State-Based Conflicts on Home Soil

Three-quarters of countries have had one or more state-based armed conflicts within their own borders since 1946.

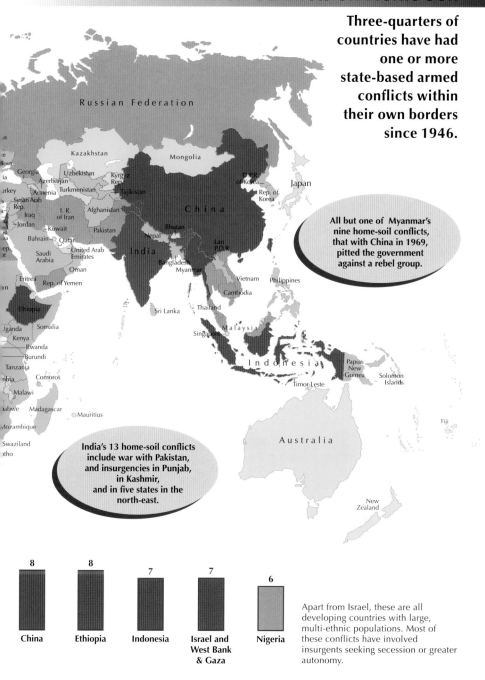

All but one of Myanmar's nine home-soil conflicts, that with China in 1969, pitted the government against a rebel group.

India's 13 home-soil conflicts include war with Pakistan, and insurgencies in Punjab, in Kashmir, and in five states in the north-east.

China	Ethiopia	Indonesia	Israel and West Bank & Gaza	Nigeria
8	8	7	7	6

Apart from Israel, these are all developing countries with large, multi-ethnic populations. Most of these conflicts have involved insurgents seeking secession or greater autonomy.

YEARS IN CONFLICT

Total number of years
in which a country has been
involved in at least one conflict
1946–2005

- 30 or more
- 15 – 29
- 5 – 14
- 1 – 4
- 0
- no data

The UK has been
engaged in an armed conflict,
at home or abroad,
for four years out of every five
since 1946.

As with other struggles
for independence, Algeria's
nine years of anti-colonial
warfare are not shown
on the map.

Canada

United States

Norway

Sweden

United Kingdom

Denmark

Ireland

The Netherlands

Rus. Fed.

Germany

Cz. Rep.

A.

Sl.

C.

M.

Italy

Portugal

Spain

Tunisia

Morocco

Algeria

Li.

Mexico

Cuba

Jamaica

Haiti

Dominican Rep.

Mauritania

Mali

Niger

Ch.

Guatemala

El Salvador

Honduras

Nicaragua

Costa Rica

Panama

Trinidad and Tobago

R. B. de Venezuela

Guyana

Senegal

The Gambia

Guinea-Bissau

Guinea

Sierra Leone

Liberia

Burkina Faso

Côte d'Ivoire

Ghana

Togo

Benin

Nigeria

Cameroon

Equatorial Guinea

Gabon

Colombia

Ecuador

Peru

Brazil

Rep. Congo

An.

Bolivia

Paraguay

Chile

Uruguay

Argentina

Nami.

Botswana

So. Af.

In spite of the worldwide
decline in armed conflict, the
overwhelming majority of
human beings aged over 60
have lived through at least
one period in which their
government was actively
engaged in armed conflict.
The countries shown in red
on the map have spent more
years in conflict than at
peace. Only conflicts
involving government forces
have been counted, and
counts started only when a
state became independent,
so the sometimes bitter years
of fighting for independence
from colonial rule are not
included.

STATES MOST OFTEN IN COMBAT

Countries with the highest
number of years in conflict
1946–2005

Israel	Myanmar	Philippines	UK
58	57	50	49

Time Spent in Conflict

Only 21 of the world's states have been entirely free from state-based armed conflicts since World War II.

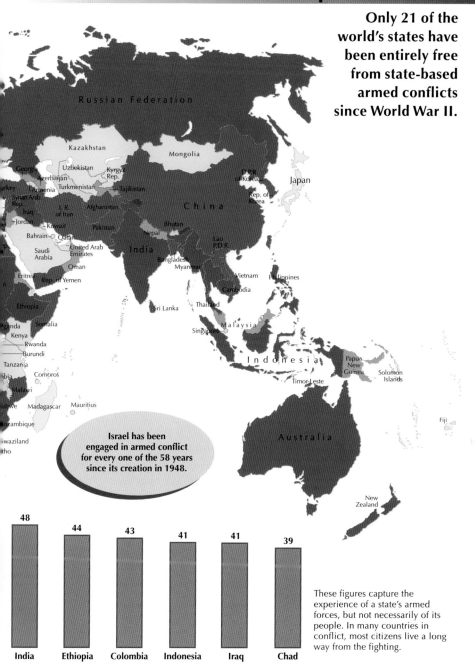

Russian Federation

Kazakhstan

Mongolia

Georgia
Uzbekistan
Kyrgyz Rep.
Azerbaijan
Turkmenistan
Armenia
Tajikistan
D.P.R. of Korea
Japan

Syrian Arab Rep.
I.R. of Iran
Afghanistan
China
Rep. of Korea

Iraq
Jordan
Kuwait
Pakistan
Bhutan

Bahrain
Qatar
Nepal

Saudi Arabia
United Arab Emirates
India
Lao P.D.R.

Oman
Bangladesh
Myanmar

Eritrea
Rep. of Yemen
Vietnam
Philippines

Cambodia

Ethiopia
Sri Lanka
Thailand

Uganda
Somalia
Kenya
Malaysia

Rwanda
Singapore

Burundi

Tanzania

Comoros
Indonesia
Papua New Guinea
Solomon Islands

Malawi

Timor-Leste

Madagascar
Mauritius

Mozambique

Swaziland
Fiji

Australia

Israel has been engaged in armed conflict for every one of the 58 years since its creation in 1948.

New Zealand

48	44	43	41	41	39
India	Ethiopia	Colombia	Indonesia	Iraq	Chad

These figures capture the experience of a state's armed forces, but not necessarily of its people. In many countries in conflict, most citizens live a long way from the fighting.

2

Warlords and Killing Fields

As well as conflicts involving governments, there are two other major forms of political violence: *non-state conflicts*, which are fought between militias, warlords, and ethnic or religious groups, without the involvement of a government, and *one-sided violence*, which includes genocides and other mass killings of defenseless civilians.

If a city or a village turns into a war zone, it makes little difference to the victims whether the perpetrators are foreign soldiers, government forces or local militia. But to understand global patterns of political violence, such distinctions are crucial.

Until very recently, there were no reliable records of non-state conflicts. To fill this gap, Uppsala University in Sweden has produced a new set of figures for the *Human Security Report*. These statistics, so far covering 2002 to 2005, confirm that the previously unrecorded non-state conflicts are almost as numerous as the state-based conflicts on which global conflict analysis used to rely exclusively. Between 2002 and 2005, there were on average 30 non-state conflicts per year, compared with 31 state-based conflicts.

Non-state conflicts tend to occur in poor countries with weak governments – from 2002 to 2005, most of them were in Sub-Saharan Africa. But they are much less deadly; battle-deaths in non-state conflicts are a quarter of those in state-based conflicts.

Are non-state conflicts, like state-based conflicts, decreasing in number? We cannot be sure, because four years is too short a period over which to detect trends with any reliability, and no one has any reliable statistics for longer than that. But non-state conflicts remained more-or-less steady from 2002 to 2005 in all regions of the world, except for Sub-Saharan Africa, where they fell sharply.

The third major type of organized killing is what the experts call "one-sided violence." This refers not to fighting between armed groups, but to the deliberate massacre of unarmed people, perpetrated either by non-state militias or by government forces.

One-sided violence includes genocide, which is defined by international law as "acts committed with the intent to destroy, in

Nepal
Tomas van
Houtryve /
Panos Pictures

whole or in part, a national, ethnical, racial or religious group." Such crimes often occur during or immediately after a civil war. In practice, it is hard to judge the *intent* of one-sided violence, as is shown by the controversy over whether or not the killings in Darfur (Sudan) qualify as genocide.

The legal definition of genocide includes massacring people for their religious beliefs, but not for their politics. On that basis, the 1975–79 killings in Cambodia under Pol Pot, in which several million Cambodians perished, were not genocide except where they targeted religious and ethnic groups. Some experts use the term *politicide* to describe deliberate slaughter aimed at a group defined by its political views.

A count by the US-based Political Instability Task Force (PITF) of genocides, politicides, and similar mass slaughters shows that the number increased tenfold from the mid-1950s to the mid-1970s, remained roughly steady until 1989, and then declined sharply.

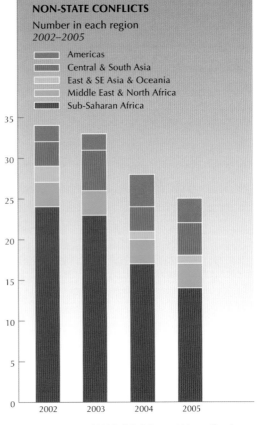

NON-STATE CONFLICTS
Number in each region
2002–2005

- Americas
- Central & South Asia
- East & SE Asia & Oceania
- Middle East & North Africa
- Sub-Saharan Africa

Between 2002 and 2005, Sub-Saharan Africa suffered well over half of the armed conflicts that did not involve a government.

Uppsala University has made a separate count of all significant deadly campaigns directed at civilians, irrespective of whether or not they were genocides or politicides. The Uppsala figures only start from 1989, but they show a clear, though uneven, upward trend over the last 17 years.

Which picture is correct? The answer is that both are – for they are not counting the same things. The PITF figures are limited to campaigns killing thousands, while the Uppsala counts include all campaigns involving 25 or more deaths in a year. So, since the end of the Cold War, genocides and other large-scale killings of civilians have indeed declined in number, but small-scale campaigns of one-sided violence have increased.

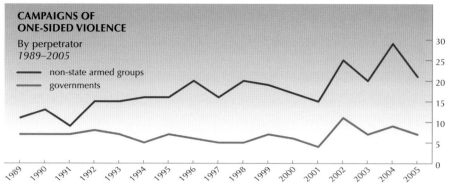

CAMPAIGNS OF ONE-SIDED VIOLENCE

By perpetrator
1989–2005

— non-state armed groups
— governments

More than two-thirds of deadly campaigns against unarmed civilians between 2002 and 2005 were perpetrated by non-state forces.

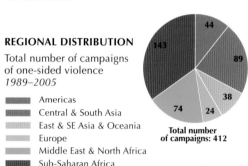

REGIONAL DISTRIBUTION

Total number of campaigns
of one-sided violence
1989–2005

- Americas
- Central & South Asia
- East & SE Asia & Oceania
- Europe
- Middle East & North Africa
- Sub-Saharan Africa

Total number of campaigns: 412

Sub-Saharan Africa, the Middle East & North Africa, and Central & South Asia suffered 74% of the campaigns of one-sided violence between 1989 and 2005. The total number of campaigns has been rising in recent years.

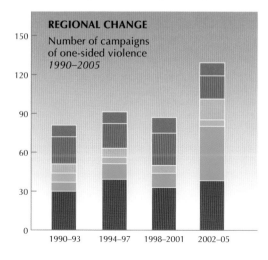

REGIONAL CHANGE

Number of campaigns
of one-sided violence
1990–2005

The Uppsala figures show that while the number of campaigns of one-sided violence by governments has remained steady, campaigns by insurgents, warlords, and militias have doubled. Of 412 such events logged by Uppsala between 1989 and 2005, three-quarters were in three regions of the world: 35% in Sub-Saharan Africa, 22% in Central & South Asia, and another 18% in the Middle East & North Africa. The remaining quarter was shared among the Americas, East & Southeast Asia & Oceania, and Europe. From 2002 onwards, there was a sharp increase in violent campaigns against civilians in the Middle East & North Africa, notably in Iraq and Sudan. The other regions showed no clear trends.

The next section of this atlas looks at death tolls and compares the number of people who die in the three main forms of organized killing: state-based conflicts, non-state conflicts, and one-sided violence.

The number of years in which
a country has experienced
at least one non-state conflict
2002–05

- 4
- 3
- 2
- 1
- 0
- no data

Canada

United States

Mexico

Cuba
Jamaica Haiti Dominican Rep.

Guatemala
El Salvador
Nicaragua
Costa Rica
Panama

Honduras

Trinidad and Tobago

R. B. de Venezuela

Colombia

Guyana

Ecuador

Peru

Brazil

Bolivia

Chile Paraguay

Uruguay

Argentina

Norway

United Kingdom
Ireland

Sweden
Denmark
The Neth. Rus. Fe
Germany Po
Bel.
Lux.
Cz.
Rep.
Sl
France S G A
Italy M
A

Portugal Spain

Morocco

Tunisia

Algeria Lib

Mauritania Mali Niger

Senegal
The Gambia
Guinea-Bissau
Guinea
Sierra Leone
Liberia

Burkina
Faso
Côte
d'Ivoire
Ghana
Togo
Benin

Ch

Nigeria

C

Cameroon
Equatorial
Guinea Gabon

Rep. Congo

An

Nami

Botswa

About half of all conflicts do
not involve the armed forces
of any government, but are
fought between various
guerrilla groups and ethnic or
religious militias. Until
recently, there were no
reliable global data for these
non-state conflicts, which
tend to be shorter and less
deadly than state-based
conflicts. The *Human
Security Report* now
publishes annual figures, but
the counts only go back to
2002. When government
forces fail to suppress armed
groups, it is a sign of limited
state capacity. At present, all
non-state conflicts take place
in developing countries.

In 2002,
the Democratic Republic of Congo
experienced five non-state conflicts.
By 2005, there were none.

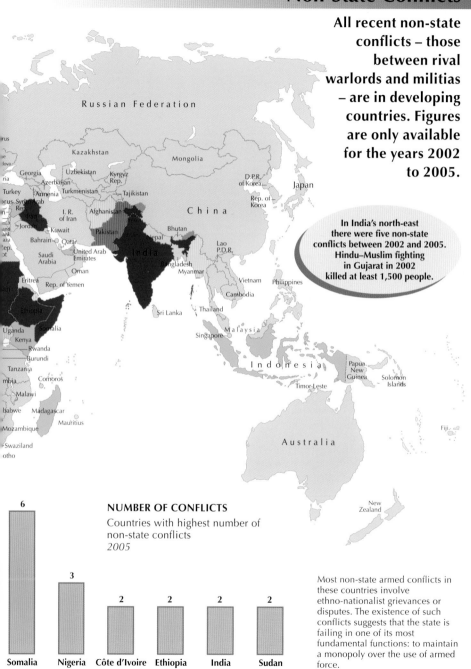

All recent non-state conflicts – those between rival warlords and militias – are in developing countries. Figures are only available for the years 2002 to 2005.

In India's north-east there were five non-state conflicts between 2002 and 2005. Hindu–Muslim fighting in Gujarat in 2002 killed at least 1,500 people.

NUMBER OF CONFLICTS
Countries with highest number of non-state conflicts
2005

6	3	2	2	2	2
Somalia	Nigeria	Côte d'Ivoire	Ethiopia	India	Sudan

Most non-state armed conflicts in these countries involve ethno-nationalist grievances or disputes. The existence of such conflicts suggests that the state is failing in one of its most fundamental functions: to maintain a monopoly over the use of armed force.

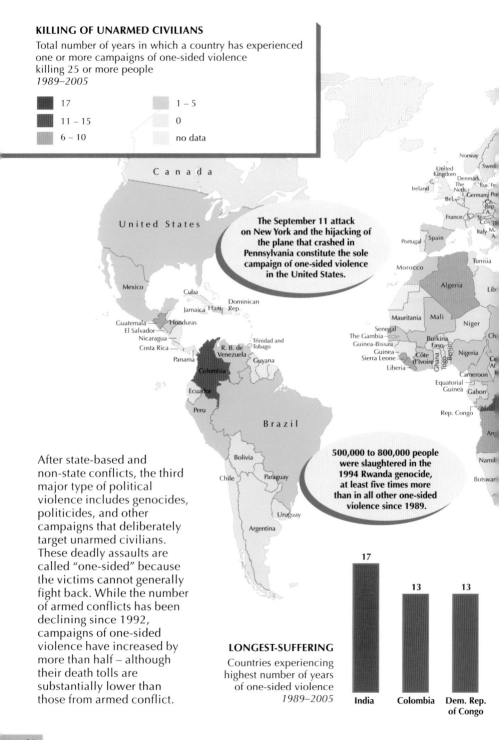

KILLING OF UNARMED CIVILIANS

Total number of years in which a country has experienced one or more campaigns of one-sided violence killing 25 or more people
1989–2005

- 17
- 11 – 15
- 6 – 10
- 1 – 5
- 0
- no data

The September 11 attack on New York and the hijacking of the plane that crashed in Pennsylvania constitute the sole campaign of one-sided violence in the United States.

500,000 to 800,000 people were slaughtered in the 1994 Rwanda genocide, at least five times more than in all other one-sided violence since 1989.

After state-based and non-state conflicts, the third major type of political violence includes genocides, politicides, and other campaigns that deliberately target unarmed civilians. These deadly assaults are called "one-sided" because the victims cannot generally fight back. While the number of armed conflicts has been declining since 1992, campaigns of one-sided violence have increased by more than half – although their death tolls are substantially lower than those from armed conflict.

LONGEST-SUFFERING

Countries experiencing highest number of years of one-sided violence
1989–2005

India	Colombia	Dem. Rep. of Congo
17	13	13

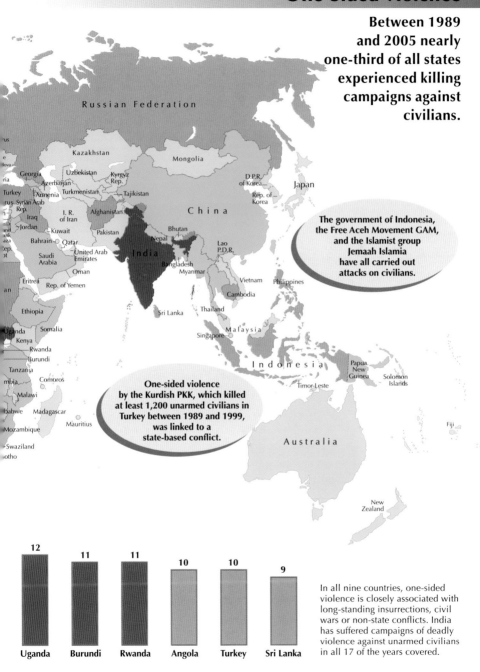

One-Sided Violence

Between 1989 and 2005 nearly one-third of all states experienced killing campaigns against civilians.

Russian Federation

Kazakhstan

Mongolia

D.P.R. of Korea

Japan

Rep. of Korea

Georgia · Uzbekistan · Kyrgyz Rep.

Azerbaijan · Turkmenistan · Tajikistan

Turkey · Armenia

Syrian Arab Rep.

Iraq · I. R. of Iran · Afghanistan

Jordan · Kuwait · Pakistan

Bahrain · Qatar

United Arab Emirates

Saudi Arabia

Oman

China

Bhutan

Nepal

India

Bangladesh

Lao P.D.R.

Myanmar

Vietnam

Cambodia

Philippines

Eritrea · Rep. of Yemen

Ethiopia

Somalia

Uganda · Kenya

Rwanda

Burundi

Tanzania

Comoros

Malawi

Madagascar

Mauritius

Mozambique

Swaziland

Sri Lanka

Thailand

Malaysia

Singapore

Indonesia

Timor-Leste

Papua New Guinea

Solomon Islands

Fiji

Australia

New Zealand

The government of Indonesia, the Free Aceh Movement GAM, and the Islamist group Jemaah Islamia have all carried out attacks on civilians.

One-sided violence by the Kurdish PKK, which killed at least 1,200 unarmed civilians in Turkey between 1989 and 1999, was linked to a state-based conflict.

12	11	11	10	10	9
Uganda	Burundi	Rwanda	Angola	Turkey	Sri Lanka

In all nine countries, one-sided violence is closely associated with long-standing insurrections, civil wars or non-state conflicts. India has suffered campaigns of deadly violence against unarmed civilians in all 17 of the years covered.

Counting the Dead

The decline in battle-deaths has been even more remarkable than the fall in the number of armed conflicts. In wars involving a state, for every 30 people killed in 1950, only one was killed in 2005. But how accurate are the death-toll statistics?

While the number of wars, conflicts, genocides and other slaughters of civilians is relatively well-documented, the deaths that result from them are difficult to count. On the world's battlegrounds and killing fields, there is little accurate book-keeping.

Some bodies are never found. The commander of an organized army knows how many of his own soldiers remain after a battle, but he cannot be sure if those missing have been killed or have deserted; leaders of hastily recruited militias and fast-moving guerrilla bands are even less certain. Military units rarely count enemy or civilian dead. And massacres of civilians are not usually documented, with many victims deliberately made to "disappear."

In all three forms of organized political violence – state-based, non-state and one-sided – the perpetrators and others often lie. One group may exaggerate deaths on its own side to demonstrate the enemy's brutality. Another may understate its casualties to appear stronger than it really is. But for policymakers, absolute numbers are not essential. What matters is that death counts can be compared – year by year, conflict by conflict, country by country. Without such evidence, there is no objective way of evaluating long-term policies or one-off interventions, or of establishing whether economic sanctions, ceasefires or peacekeeping missions are effective.

Until recently, no such comprehensive numbers existed for non-state conflict and one-sided violence. But the University of Uppsala recently completed a new set of global figures for the *Human Security Report* which counts "reported deaths" from all three main forms of organized violence. This dataset does not provide a true measure of total deaths. Rather, it is a careful count of only those fatalities that satisfy a series of strict, consistent and published criteria. In essence, these are minimum figures. Uppsala follows three basic rules in counting deaths. First, a death must be documented by a reasonably

Angola
J.B. Russell /
Panos Pictures

reliable source. Second, there must be enough evidence to attribute a death to a specific conflict, or to a specific campaign of political killing. Third, the conflict or campaign must have caused at least 25 deaths in a calendar year.

These stringent criteria mean that Uppsala's annual counts of "reported deaths" are almost invariably lower – sometimes far lower – than the real death tolls, especially for one-sided violence. But year by year and conflict by conflict, data are now being collected using the same standard criteria – data that can be used with confidence to explore three key issues: the year-on-year trends, the relative deadliness of the three main forms of organized political violence, and the geographical spread.

Battle-deaths in state-based armed conflicts have been on a downward trend since the late 1960s. Deaths from non-state conflicts dropped by more than two-thirds from 2002 to 2005, although four years is much too short a time to draw firm conclusions about trends.

Between 1989 and 2005, the only years for which we have figures, there is no clear trend in deaths from one-sided violence. Fatalities from this form of organized political violence are especially difficult to record accurately, as has been evident recently in Darfur (Sudan) and Iraq.

Most deaths from organized political violence are in armed conflicts involving states – 69 percent in 2005. Three regions – Central & South Asia, the Middle East & North Africa, and Sub-Saharan Africa – accounted for nearly 80 percent of battle-deaths in state-based conflicts in 2005. For non-state conflicts, the pattern was different, with more than 40 percent of battle-deaths occurring in Sub-Saharan Africa. And for one-sided violence, almost half of all deaths were in the Middle East & North Africa, where attacks in Iraq and Darfur (Sudan) drove up the death tolls.

One widely publicized form of violence against civilians – terrorism –

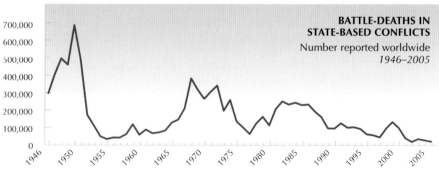

BATTLE-DEATHS IN STATE-BASED CONFLICTS
Number reported worldwide
1946–2005

The peak in 1950 was caused by the Korean War, and the peak in 1968 is associated with the Vietnam War. Overall there has been a dramatic decrease in battle-deaths since World War II.

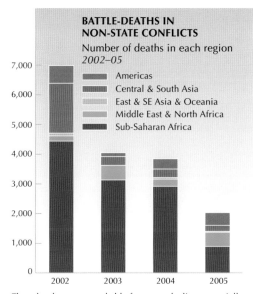

BATTLE-DEATHS IN NON-STATE CONFLICTS

Number of deaths in each region
2002–05

- Americas
- Central & South Asia
- East & SE Asia & Oceania
- Middle East & North Africa
- Sub-Saharan Africa

There has been a remarkable four-year decline, especially in Sub-Saharan Africa and Central & South Asia.

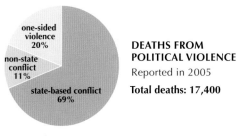

DEATHS FROM POLITICAL VIOLENCE

Reported in 2005

Total deaths: 17,400

one-sided violence 20%

non-state conflict 11%

state-based conflict 69%

is not separately identified in these statistics. This is because there is no widespread agreement on what distinguishes it from other forms of organized violence. "Terrorism" is often used to describe acts of insurgency. And many consider acts of government-instigated one-sided mass violence to be "state terrorism." Most deaths from "terrorism" are, however, included in one of the three main types of organized violence in the Uppsala totals.

With data now being collected on death tolls from non-state conflicts and one-sided violence, our understanding of the true human costs of war has greatly improved. Although such death tolls generally represent minimum totals, they enable comparisons between regions and over time. But, as the next section of this atlas shows, there is far less information on other human rights abuses.

DEATHS FROM POLITICAL VIOLENCE IN EACH REGION

2005

- Americas
- Central & South Asia
- East & SE Asia & Oceania
- Europe
- Middle East & North Africa
- Sub-Saharan Africa

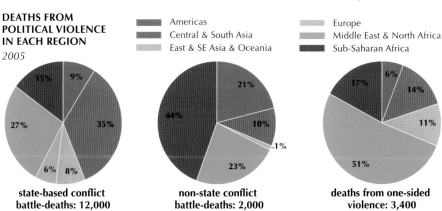

state-based conflict battle-deaths: 12,000

15% 9% 35% 27% 6% 8%

non-state conflict battle-deaths: 2,000

21% 44% 10% 1% 23%

deaths from one-sided violence: 3,400

6% 17% 14% 11% 51%

While useful for tracking trends, these figures underestimate the real death tolls. This is particularly true in the case of Iraq, where fatality estimates are wildly divergent and intensely controversial.

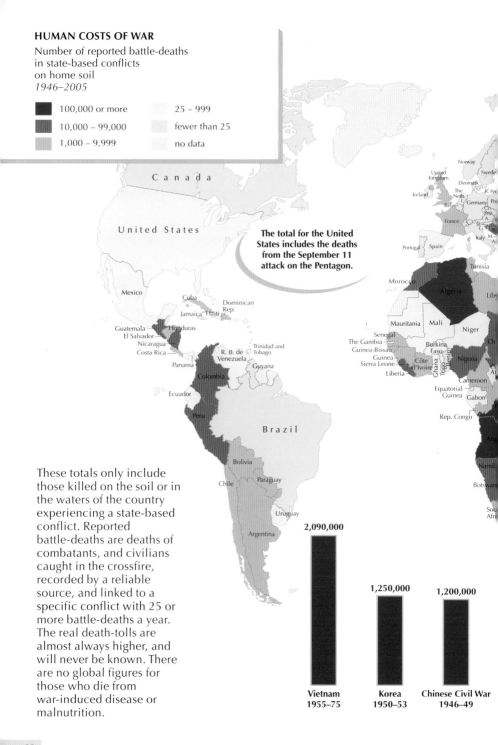

HUMAN COSTS OF WAR

Number of reported battle-deaths
in state-based conflicts
on home soil
1946–2005

- 100,000 or more
- 10,000 – 99,000
- 1,000 – 9,999
- 25 – 999
- fewer than 25
- no data

The total for the United
States includes the deaths
from the September 11
attack on the Pentagon.

These totals only include
those killed on the soil or in
the waters of the country
experiencing a state-based
conflict. Reported
battle-deaths are deaths of
combatants, and civilians
caught in the crossfire,
recorded by a reliable
source, and linked to a
specific conflict with 25 or
more battle-deaths a year.
The real death-tolls are
almost always higher, and
will never be known. There
are no global figures for
those who die from
war-induced disease or
malnutrition.

2,090,000	1,250,000	1,200,000
Vietnam 1955–75	**Korea** 1950–53	**Chinese Civil War** 1946–49

Battle-Deaths in State-Based Conflicts

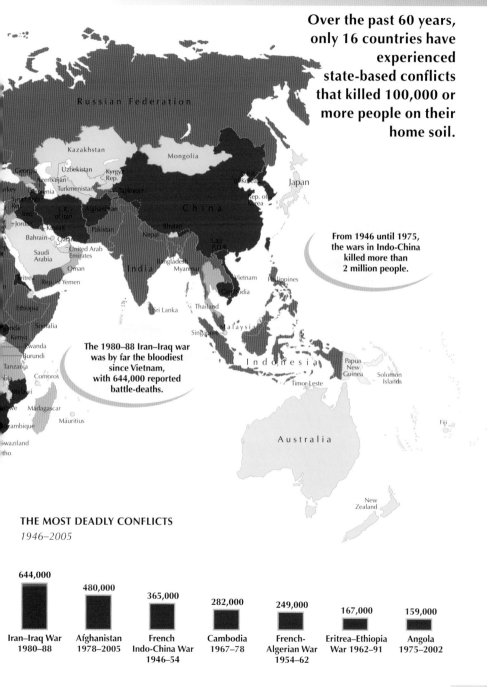

Over the past 60 years, only 16 countries have experienced state-based conflicts that killed 100,000 or more people on their home soil.

From 1946 until 1975, the wars in Indo-China killed more than 2 million people.

The 1980–88 Iran–Iraq war was by far the bloodiest since Vietnam, with 644,000 reported battle-deaths.

THE MOST DEADLY CONFLICTS

1946–2005

644,000	480,000	365,000	282,000	249,000	167,000	159,000
Iran–Iraq War 1980–88	Afghanistan 1978–2005	French Indo-China War 1946–54	Cambodia 1967–78	French-Algerian War 1954–62	Eritrea–Ethiopia War 1962–91	Angola 1975–2002

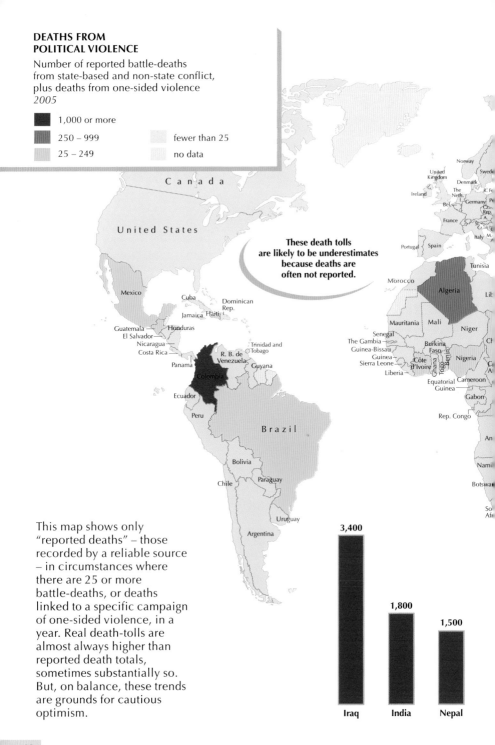

DEATHS FROM POLITICAL VIOLENCE

Number of reported battle-deaths
from state-based and non-state conflict,
plus deaths from one-sided violence
2005

- 1,000 or more
- 250 – 999
- 25 – 249
- fewer than 25
- no data

**These death tolls
are likely to be underestimates
because deaths are
often not reported.**

This map shows only "reported deaths" – those recorded by a reliable source – in circumstances where there are 25 or more battle-deaths, or deaths linked to a specific campaign of one-sided violence, in a year. Real death-tolls are almost always higher than reported death totals, sometimes substantially so. But, on balance, these trends are grounds for cautious optimism.

3,400 — Iraq
1,800 — India
1,500 — Nepal

Deaths from Political Violence

Although warfare remains common, the great majority of people live in countries free of all forms of deadly political violence.

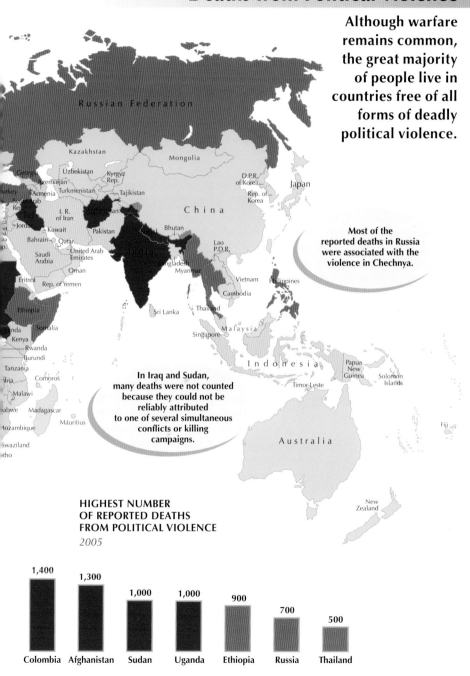

Most of the reported deaths in Russia were associated with the violence in Chechnya.

In Iraq and Sudan, many deaths were not counted because they could not be reliably attributed to one of several simultaneous conflicts or killing campaigns.

HIGHEST NUMBER OF REPORTED DEATHS FROM POLITICAL VIOLENCE
2005

Colombia	Afghanistan	Sudan	Uganda	Ethiopia	Russia	Thailand
1,400	1,300	1,000	1,000	900	700	500

4

> Ethnic cleansing, death squads, child soldiers and other extreme assaults on human rights are not uncommon, but there are almost no reliable global figures.

Measuring Human Rights Abuse

Rape, burned villages, and poisoned wells have long been associated with warfare and rebellion. And torture and concentration camps are widely used by dictatorships to impose order on the streets. What are the long-term trends, and can we make reliable comparisons between countries?

Some of the worst human rights violations take place in secret. Certain governments, for example, admit they deliberately inflict pain to extract information from suspects. But they do not publish annual reports, or allow independent observers into their torture chambers. Most human rights organizations do not collect statistics even on the worst cruelties, in case this implies that abusing one person is more acceptable than abusing a hundred. But without quantitative annual audits, such as those now available for wars and genocides, it is hard to devise policies against rights violations, or to evaluate whether those policies are effective.

Child soldiers (aged under 18, according to international law) represent one human rights abuse that has been widely publicized. Children are recruited into both rebel and government forces, to become sentries, spies, killers of civilians, clearers of minefields, or sex slaves. Many are under 14, and 40 percent are said to be girls.

Child soldiers are cheap, obedient, plentiful, and treated as expendable. It is a high-risk occupation, with an estimated 100,000 Iranian child soldiers killed during the 1980–88 Iran–Iraq War. Yet there are no reliable global figures on their use. The widely reported total of 300,000 worldwide first appeared in 1996, but with no indication of how it was calculated. It was quoted in a UN report, and is still being uncritically recycled as a "UN figure." Even if it was approximately correct ten years ago, the total has almost certainly fallen since, because today there are significantly fewer conflicts, and some of those that most notoriously employed child soldiers have now ended.

Albania
Andrew Testa /
Panos Pictures

The same lack of convincing and reliable figures applies to death squads, the "disappeared" and nearly all other gross human rights abuses. There is little solid information on country-by-country occurrence, the numbers involved, or trends over time.

Two yardsticks – refugees and the Political Terror Scale – may reflect, but cannot measure, the sum total of all these various human rights violations. Violence and abuse may force people to flee their homes. If they cross a national border, they become refugees, and if they escape within their own countries, they are "internally displaced persons" (IDPs). The global number of refugees and IDPs rose tenfold in the 30 years from the mid-1960s. Then, after the decline in armed conflicts at the end of the Cold War, they started to fall. But while refugee totals continued to drop, IDP numbers increased sharply from 1998 to 2002, and have changed little since. It is not clear why.

However, refugee and IDP numbers are at best an indirect indication of the combined effect of many different human rights violations. An authoritarian state may prevent people leaving home, and it can be hard to distinguish refugees from economic migrants.

The Political Terror Scale (PTS) from the University of North Carolina uses Amnesty International and US State Department annual reports to rank countries on a five-point scale – from Level 1 (secure rule of law, no political prisoners, torture rare) to Level 5 (political murder, brutality, and terror with a nationwide impact). But the PTS scores are based on subjective judgments that may have become stricter over the decades, so the level of repression in recent years is possibly lower than the trend lines indicate.

DISPLACED PEOPLE

Total number of refugees and IDPs by region of origin
2005

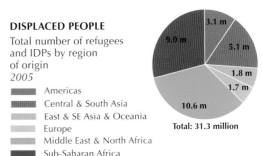

████ Americas
████ Central & South Asia
████ East & SE Asia & Oceania
████ Europe
████ Middle East & North Africa
████ Sub-Saharan Africa

Almost two-thirds of the world's displaced people are from Sub-Saharan Africa and the Middle East & North Africa.

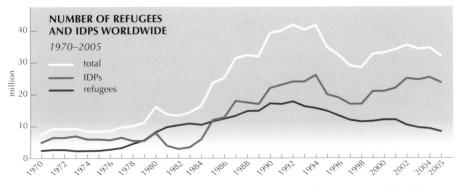

NUMBER OF REFUGEES AND IDPS WORLDWIDE

1970–2005

Between 1998 and 2005, the number of refugees (displaced persons who cross a national border) declined, while the number of IDPs (internally displaced persons) increased.

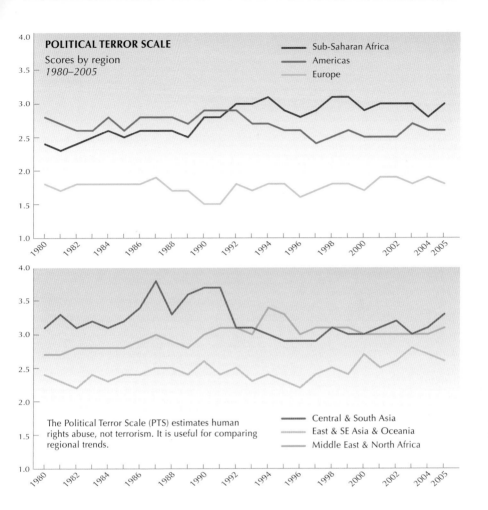

POLITICAL TERROR SCALE
Scores by region
1980–2005

Sub-Saharan Africa
Americas
Europe

The Political Terror Scale (PTS) estimates human rights abuse, not terrorism. It is useful for comparing regional trends.

Central & South Asia
East & SE Asia & Oceania
Middle East & North Africa

There are two other ways of identifying the countries where human rights abuses are pervasive. The first is by counting deaths from political violence per 100,000 people, and the second is by using a World Bank index of the estimated risk that violence will destabilize a government. Together, these three very different methods can be used to identify with some confidence where human rights are most outrageously violated. But with respect to specific abuses, the available figures are inadequate and incomplete.

It is clear that human rights are better respected in democracies than under authoritarian regimes. The next section of this atlas looks at the causes of armed conflict, and explores what types of government are most likely to go to war.

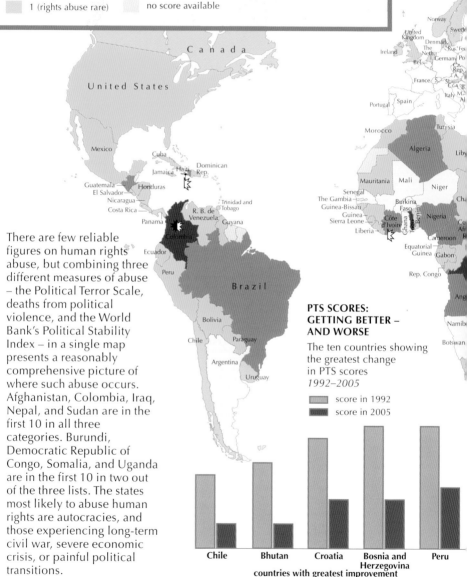

INDICATORS OF HUMAN RIGHTS ABUSE

Score on Political Terror Scale
2005

- 4.5 – 5 (high level of abuse)
- 3.5 – 4
- 2.5 – 3
- 1.5 – 2
- 1 (rights abuse rare)
- no score available

➤ one of the 10 countries with most deaths from political violence per 100,000 population, *2005*

⧖ one of the 10 countries with worst scores in the World Bank Political Stability & Absence of Violence Index, *2005*

There are few reliable figures on human rights abuse, but combining three different measures of abuse – the Political Terror Scale, deaths from political violence, and the World Bank's Political Stability Index – in a single map presents a reasonably comprehensive picture of where such abuse occurs. Afghanistan, Colombia, Iraq, Nepal, and Sudan are in the first 10 in all three categories. Burundi, Democratic Republic of Congo, Somalia, and Uganda are in the first 10 in two out of the three lists. The states most likely to abuse human rights are autocracies, and those experiencing long-term civil war, severe economic crisis, or painful political transitions.

PTS SCORES: GETTING BETTER – AND WORSE

The ten countries showing the greatest change in PTS scores
1992–2005

- score in 1992
- score in 2005

Chile Bhutan Croatia Bosnia and Herzegovina Peru

countries with greatest improvement

Human Rights Abuse

Measuring human rights abuse is difficult, controversial, and rarely attempted on a global scale. But three quite different measures provide some insight into the scope of the problem.

Russian Federation

Kazakhstan

Mongolia

Georgia
Uzbekistan
Kyrgyz Rep.
D.P.R. of Korea
Japan

Azerbaijan
Turkmenistan
Tajikistan
Rep. of Korea

Turkey
Armenia
Syrian Arab Rep.
I. R. of Iran
Afghanistan
China

Iraq
Jordan
Kuwait
Pakistan
Nepal
Bhutan

Bahrain
Qatar
Lao P.D.R.

Saudi Arabia
United Arab Emirates
Bangladesh
Myanmar

Oman
India
Vietnam
Philippines

Eritrea
Rep. of Yemen
Cambodia

Ethiopia
Sri Lanka
Thailand

Uganda
Somalia
Malaysia

Kenya
Singapore

Rwanda
Indonesia
Papua New Guinea
Solomon Islands

Burundi

Tanzania
Comoros
Timor-Leste

Malawi

Mozambique
Fiji

Swaziland
Australia

Lesotho

> Comoros and Bhutan are the only low-income countries to get the best possible PTS score. The US and UK have the worst scores among high-income countries.

New Zealand

political murder and brutality widespread

5

4

3

2

1

0 rights abuse rare

Uzbekistan | Israel | Zimbabwe | Togo | Nepal

countries with greatest deterioration

The five states with scores that deteriorated all underwent severe political or economic crises, or became more authoritarian.

CHILD SOLDIERS

Ratification of the 1989 UN Convention on the Rights of the Child (CRC) and the 2002 Optional Protocol on Children in Armed Conflict (OPCAC).
December 2005

- ratified CRC only
- ratified OPCAC only
- ratified both
- ratified neither
- no data

Child soldiers used in active combat
2001–04

- ☐ governments used child soldiers
- ✗ non-state armed groups used child soldiers
- ☒ governments and non-state armed groups used child soldiers

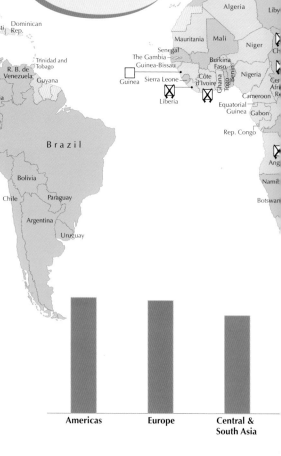

The USA is known to have deployed a small number of soldiers aged under 18 to Iraq.

Because there are few reliable figures, the map understates the recent use of child soldiers. International law on the subject is not robust. The CRC (see above) allows the recruitment of soldiers aged under 18, but not under 15. OPCAC prohibits non-state armed groups from using under-18s as soldiers. The state is forbidden to recruit them compulsorily, but can accept voluntary recruits. Only the USA and Somalia have not ratified the CRC, and most states have ratified OPCAC. Of the 12 African governments that used child soldiers between 2001 and 2004, five have ratified both treaties.

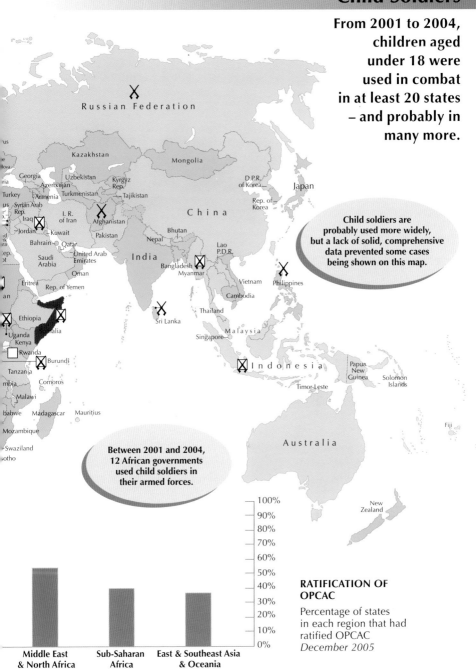

Child Soldiers

From 2001 to 2004, children aged under 18 were used in combat in at least 20 states – and probably in many more.

Russian Federation

Kazakhstan

Mongolia

Georgia
Uzbekistan
Kyrgyz Rep.
D.P.R. of Korea
Japan

Azerbaijan
Turkmenistan
Tajikistan

Turkey
Armenia
Rep. of Korea

Syrian Arab Rep.
Iraq
I. R. of Iran
Afghanistan
China

Jordan
Kuwait
Pakistan
Nepal
Bhutan

Bahrain
Qatar
United Arab Emirates
India
Lao P.D.R.

Saudi Arabia
Oman
Bangladesh
Myanmar
Vietnam
Philippines

Eritrea
Rep. of Yemen
Cambodia

Ethiopia
Sri Lanka
Thailand

Uganda
Somalia
Malaysia

Kenya
Singapore

Rwanda
Burundi
Indonesia
Papua New Guinea
Solomon Islands

Tanzania
Comoros
Timor-Leste

mbia
Malawi

babwe
Madagascar
Mauritius

Mozambique

Swaziland
Australia

otho

Fiji

New Zealand

> Child soldiers are probably used more widely, but a lack of solid, comprehensive data prevented some cases being shown on this map.

> Between 2001 and 2004, 12 African governments used child soldiers in their armed forces.

100%
90%
80%
70%
60%
50%
40%
30%
20%
10%
0%

RATIFICATION OF OPCAC

Percentage of states in each region that had ratified OPCAC
December 2005

| Middle East & North Africa | Sub-Saharan Africa | East & Southeast Asia & Oceania |

Causes of War, Causes of Peace

Since 1945 there have been three broad shifts in the pattern of armed conflict: the end of colonial warfare, the virtual disappearance of conflicts between states, and a rapid rise in fighting within states, followed by a steep fall.

These historic changes have been associated with two epochal events: the end of European colonialism and the end of the Cold War. After World War II, nearly all of Africa, much of Asia, and parts of Latin America were under colonial rule. By 1980, all but a few small colonies were independent. A major cause of warfare had disappeared. But what of fighting between states in the post-colonial era? And why the post-Cold War reduction in conflicts within states? Here, the answers are more complex.

The low level of post-1945 inter-state warfare has been a response to three major factors. The first was democratization: the steady rise in the proportion of democracies to dictatorships. Democracies hardly ever fight each other. Second, was globalization. It is now almost always cheaper to buy resources on the global market than to seize them by force. States have found less costly ways than war to achieve their goals. Third, global sentiment has shifted firmly away from war. Until World War I, warfare was seen as an inevitable part of human experience, and an accepted instrument of statecraft. In most (though not all) societies, this is no longer so. An increasingly war-averse world has declared acts of aggression illegal, and that armed force is only justified in self-defense, or with the authority of the Security Council. These rules are still sometimes broken, but they are increasingly accepted as legitimate.

The United Nations was established in 1945, but for nearly 50 years it rarely played the global security role that its founders envisaged. The 40-year peace between the major powers during the Cold War was linked to the mutual possession of weapons of mass destruction. But the Cold War also stoked proxy wars in many poor countries. By 1992, conflicts within states were at an all-time high.

When the Cold War ended, a major driver of armed conflict vanished. But the break-up of the Soviet Union and of Yugoslavia

Guatemala
Paul Smith/
Panos Pictures

revealed new tensions – and brought new conflicts – to the Balkans, the Caucasus, and Central Asia. Indeed, twice as many conflicts started in the 1990s as in the 1980s. But the 1990s also saw an even greater increase in the number of wars coming to an end, leading to the net decline in conflict numbers.

One explanation for this decline is the explosion in international activism, spearheaded by the UN, which took place in the wake of the Cold War. UN peacemaking missions (diplomacy to halt ongoing wars) rose from four in 1990 to 15 in 2002. UN peacekeeping operations (involving troops on the

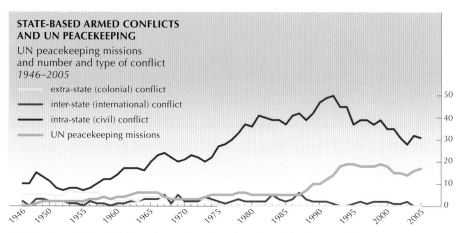

STATE-BASED ARMED CONFLICTS AND UN PEACEKEEPING

UN peacekeeping missions and number and type of conflict
1946–2005

- extra-state (colonial) conflict
- inter-state (international) conflict
- intra-state (civil) conflict
- UN peacekeeping missions

Following the end of the Cold War, the number of armed conflicts declined. During the same period the number of peacekeeping operations increased.

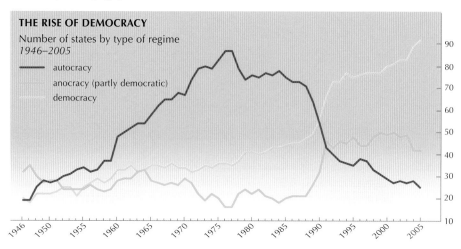

THE RISE OF DEMOCRACY

Number of states by type of regime
1946–2005

- autocracy
- anocracy (partly democratic)
- democracy

In 1975, only 26% of states were democracies. By 2005, the figure was 58%. Democracy is characterized here by constraints on the exercise of executive power, free elections and guaranteed civil liberties.

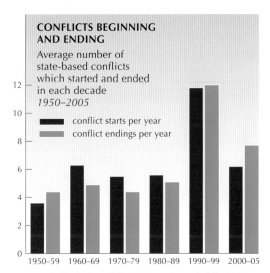

CONFLICTS BEGINNING AND ENDING

Average number of state-based conflicts which started and ended in each decade *1950–2005*

■ conflict starts per year
■ conflict endings per year

From the beginning of the 1960s to the end of the 1980s, more armed conflicts started than stopped each decade. Since then, more have ended than have begun.

ground) rose from 10 in 1990 to 17 in 2005, and have fundamentally changed in character. While the missions of the Cold War era rarely involved more than monitoring ceasefire lines, most of today's peace operations aim to rebuild national institutions and prevent the resumption of violence.

This upsurge of UN activity, backed by initiatives from regional organizations and NGOs, has often been poorly planned and implemented. But the fact that as international activism increased in the 1990s, conflicts declined, suggests – but does not prove – that the former caused the latter.

There is also an important association between armed conflict and poverty. The poor are, of course, not inherently more violent than the rich. But higher per capita income tends to mean a stronger state, which means more resources to crush rebellions or to address the grievances that drive them.

The end of the Cold War was associated with another important change. Since the beginning of the 1990s, more conflicts have ended in negotiated settlements, fewer in victories, in large part because peacemaking efforts are increasingly successful. Unfortunately, nearly 30 percent of negotiated settlements break down in under five years. This is why the UN and other international organizations are now putting so much effort into "post-conflict peacebuilding" – policies designed to prevent wars from starting up again.

Will the present downward trends in armed conflict continue? The answer depends on how successful the international community is in stopping existing wars, and in ensuring that peace agreements are durable.

INCOME AND ARMED CONFLICT

World Bank income categories
based on Gross National Income per capita
2005

- ▮ $875 or less (low)
- ▮ $876 – $3,465 (lower-middle)
- ▯ $3,466 – $10,725 (upper-middle)
- ▯ $10,726 or more (high)
- ▒ no data

**Number and type of
armed conflict**
2005

- ◖ state-based conflict
- ◗ non-state conflict

[Map of the Americas, Europe, and Africa with country labels including Canada, United States, Mexico, Guatemala, El Salvador, Nicaragua, Costa Rica, Panama, Cuba, Jamaica, Haiti, Dominican Rep., Honduras, Trinidad and Tobago, R. B. de Venezuela, Guyana, Colombia, Ecuador, Peru, Brazil, Bolivia, Chile, Paraguay, Uruguay, Argentina, Norway, United Kingdom, Ireland, Sweden, Denmark, The Neth., Bel., Germany, Cz. Rep., France, Italy, Spain, Portugal, Morocco, Tunisia, Algeria, Mauritania, Mali, Niger, Senegal, The Gambia, Guinea-Bissau, Guinea, Sierra Leone, Liberia, Burkina Faso, Nigeria, Côte d'Ivoire, Togo, Benin, Cameroon, Equatorial Guinea, Gabon, Rep. Congo, Namibia, Botswana]

There is a close association between war and poverty for several reasons. First, armed conflicts create or exacerbate poverty – war has aptly been described as "development in reverse." Second, poor countries, unlike rich ones, lack the resources to address the grievances that can spark armed uprisings. Third, poor countries tend to have weak security forces and so find it difficult to deter rebellions and to crush those that cannot be deterred.

INCOME-BANDS AND ARMED CONFLICTS

Percentage of states
in each income-band
with armed conflict
2005

- ▒ state-based conflict
- ▮ non-state conflict

19% 17%

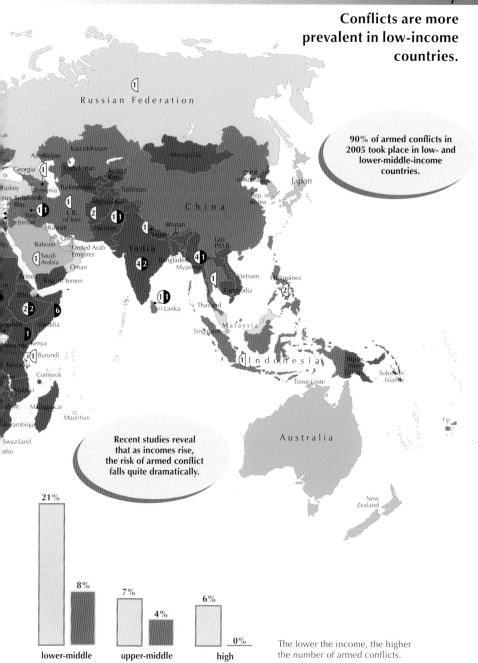

Conflicts are more prevalent in low-income countries.

90% of armed conflicts in 2005 took place in low- and lower-middle-income countries.

Recent studies reveal that as incomes rise, the risk of armed conflict falls quite dramatically.

21%

8%

7%

4%

6%

0%

lower-middle   upper-middle   high

The lower the income, the higher the number of armed conflicts.

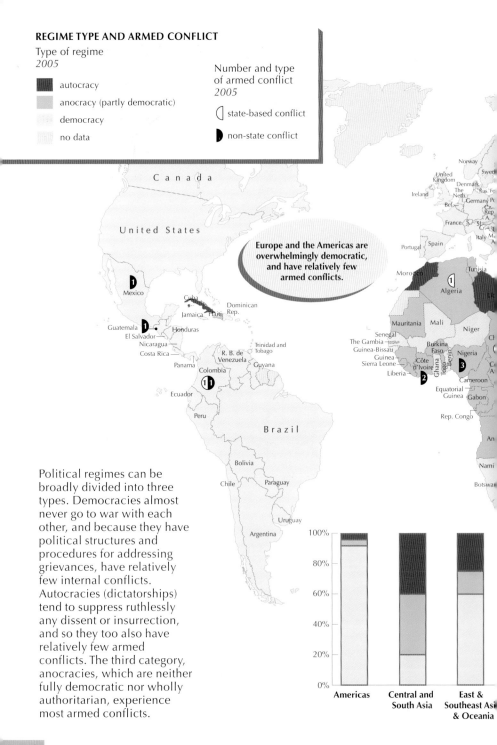

REGIME TYPE AND ARMED CONFLICT

Type of regime
2005

■ autocracy

□ anocracy (partly democratic)

□ democracy

□ no data

Number and type
of armed conflict
2005

◖ state-based conflict

◗ non-state conflict

Europe and the Americas are
overwhelmingly democratic,
and have relatively few
armed conflicts.

Canada

United States

Mexico

Cuba

Jamaica — Haiti

Dominican Rep.

Guatemala

El Salvador

Honduras

Nicaragua

Costa Rica

Panama

Trinidad and Tobago

R. B. de Venezuela

Colombia

Guyana

Ecuador

Peru

Brazil

Bolivia

Chile

Paraguay

Uruguay

Argentina

Norway

Sweden

United Kingdom

Denmark

The Neth.

Ireland

Bel.

France

Germany

Rus. Fe

Italy

Portugal

Spain

Morocco

Tunisia

Algeria

Mauritania

Mali

Niger

Senegal

The Gambia

Guinea-Bissau

Guinea

Sierra Leone

Burkina Faso

Côte d'Ivoire

Ghana

Togo

Benin

Nigeria

Liberia

Cameroon

Equatorial Guinea

Gabon

Rep. Congo

Nami

Botswa

Political regimes can be
broadly divided into three
types. Democracies almost
never go to war with each
other, and because they have
political structures and
procedures for addressing
grievances, have relatively
few internal conflicts.
Autocracies (dictatorships)
tend to suppress ruthlessly
any dissent or insurrection,
and so they too also have
relatively few armed
conflicts. The third category,
anocracies, which are neither
fully democratic nor wholly
authoritarian, experience
most armed conflicts.

100%

80%

60%

40%

20%

0%

Americas

Central and
South Asia

East &
Southeast Asia
& Oceania

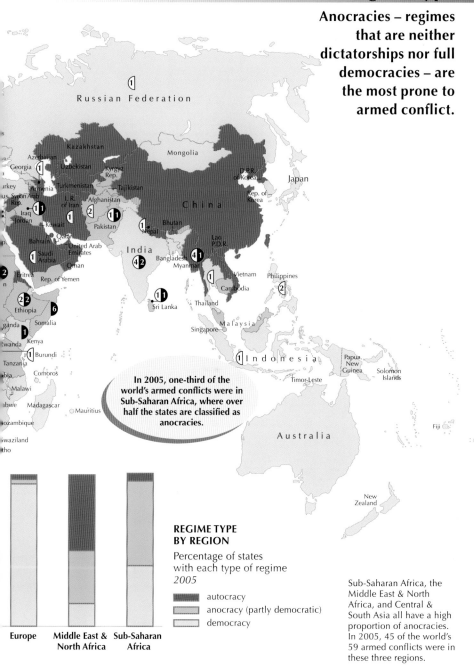

Conflict and Regime Type

Anocracies – regimes that are neither dictatorships nor full democracies – are the most prone to armed conflict.

Russian Federation ①

Kazakhstan

Mongolia

Azerbaijan

Georgia ①

Uzbekistan

Kyrgyz Rep.

D.P.R. of Korea

Japan

Armenia

Turkmenistan

Tajikistan

Rep. of Korea

urkey

us Syrian Arab Rep.

I. R. of Iran ①①

Afghanistan ②

China

Iraq

Pakistan ①①

Jordan

Kuwait

Nepal ①

Bhutan

Lao. P.D.R.

④①

Bahrain

Qatar

United Arab Emirates

India

Bangladesh ④②

Myanmar

Vietnam

Philippines ②

Saudi Arabia ①

Oman

②

Eritrea

Rep. of Yemen

Sri Lanka ①①

Thailand

Cambodia

②②

Ethiopia

⑥

Somalia

Malaysia

ganda

Kenya

Singapore

wanda

Burundi ①

Tanzania

Indonesia ①

Papua New Guinea

Solomon Islands

bia

Comoros

Timor-Leste

Malawi

abwe

Madagascar

Mauritius

Australia

ozambique

Fiji

swaziland

tho

In 2005, one-third of the world's armed conflicts were in Sub-Saharan Africa, where over half the states are classified as anocracies.

New Zealand

REGIME TYPE BY REGION

Percentage of states with each type of regime
2005

■ autocracy
■ anocracy (partly democratic)
□ democracy

| Europe | Middle East & North Africa | Sub-Saharan Africa |

Sub-Saharan Africa, the Middle East & North Africa, and Central & South Asia all have a high proportion of anocracies. In 2005, 45 of the world's 59 armed conflicts were in these three regions.

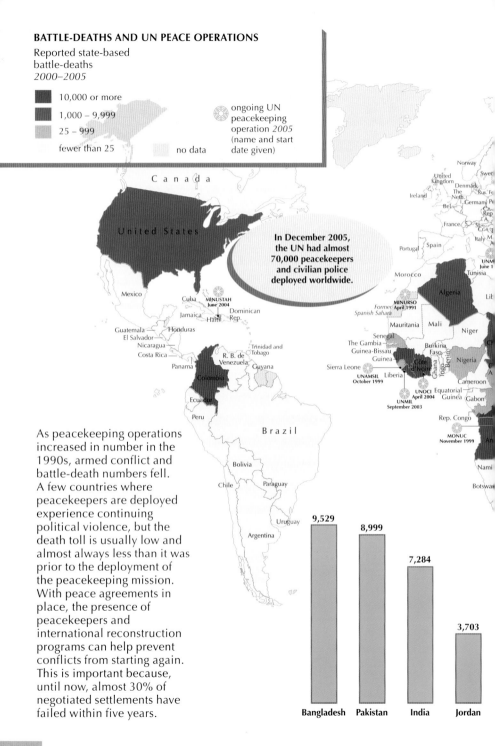

BATTLE-DEATHS AND UN PEACE OPERATIONS

Reported state-based
battle-deaths
2000–2005

- 10,000 or more
- 1,000 – 9,999
- 25 – 999
- fewer than 25

- no data

ongoing UN
peacekeeping
operation *2005*
(name and start
date given)

In December 2005,
the UN had almost
70,000 peacekeepers
and civilian police
deployed worldwide.

Canada

United States

Mexico

Cuba   MINUSTAH
June 2004

Jamaica   Dominican
Haiti   Rep.

Guatemala
El Salvador
Nicaragua
Costa Rica

Honduras

Trinidad and
Tobago

Panama

R. B. de
Venezuela

Guyana

Colombia

Ecuador

Peru

Brazil

Bolivia

Chile   Paraguay

Uruguay

Argentina

Norway

United
Kingdom   Swec
Denmark
Ireland   The   Rus. Fe
Neth.
Bel.   Germany Po
Cze.
Rep
France   Sv.
C·a   I
Italy M·a
Portugal   Spain

UNM
June 1
Tunisia

Morocco

Algeria   Lik

MINURSO
April 1991
Former Spanish Sahara

Mauritania   Mali   Niger

Senegal
The Gambia
Guinea-Bissau
Guinea

Burkina
Faso

Nigeria

Sierra Leone

UNAMSIL
October 1999

Côte
d'Ivoire

Ghana
Togo
Benin

Cameroon

Liberia

UNOCI   Equatorial
April 2004   Guinea   Gabon
UNMIL
September 2003

Rep. Congo

MONUC
November 1999   An

Nami

Botswa

As peacekeeping operations
increased in number in the
1990s, armed conflict and
battle-death numbers fell.
A few countries where
peacekeepers are deployed
experience continuing
political violence, but the
death toll is usually low and
almost always less than it was
prior to the deployment of
the peacekeeping mission.
With peace agreements in
place, the presence of
peacekeepers and
international reconstruction
programs can help prevent
conflicts from starting again.
This is important because,
until now, almost 30% of
negotiated settlements have
failed within five years.

9,529	8,999	7,284	3,703
Bangladesh	Pakistan	India	Jordan

Peacekeeping and Armed Conflict

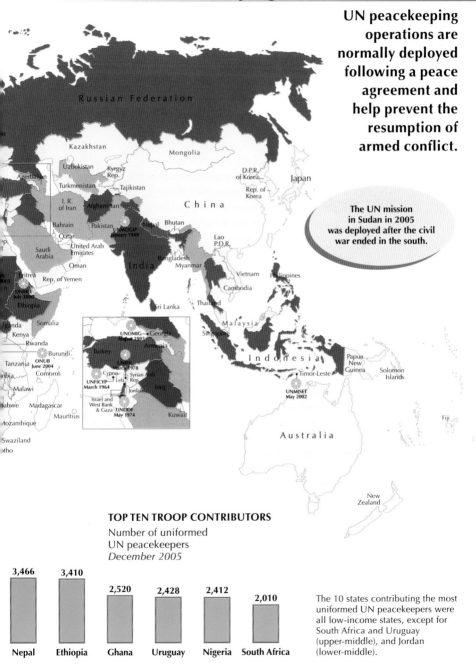

UN peacekeeping operations are normally deployed following a peace agreement and help prevent the resumption of armed conflict.

The UN mission in Sudan in 2005 was deployed after the civil war ended in the south.

Russian Federation

Kazakhstan

Mongolia

Uzbekistan

Azerbaijan
Turkmenistan
Kyrgyz Rep.
Tajikistan

D.P.R. of Korea
Japan
Rep. of Korea

I. R. of Iran
Afghanistan
Nepal
Bhutan

China

Bahrain
Qatar
Pakistan
UNMOGIP
January 1949

Lao P.D.R.

Saudi Arabia
United Arab Emirates
Oman

India
Bangladesh
Myanmar

Vietnam
Philippines

Eritrea
Rep. of Yemen
UNMEE
July 2000

Cambodia

Ethiopia
Somalia

Sri Lanka
Thailand

Malaysia
Singapore

Uganda
Kenya
Rwanda
Burundi
ONUB
June 2004

UNOMIG Georgia
August 1993
Armenia

Indonesia

Papua New Guinea
Solomon Islands

Tanzania
Comoros
Malawi

Turkey
UNIFIL
March 1978
Cyprus
Leb.
Syrian Arab Rep.
Iraq

Timor-Leste
UNMISET
May 2002

Madagascar
Mauritius
UNFICYP
March 1964

Israel and West Bank & Gaza
Jordan
UNDOF
May 1974
Kuwait

Fiji

Mozambique
Swaziland
Lesotho

Australia

New Zealand

TOP TEN TROOP CONTRIBUTORS

Number of uniformed
UN peacekeepers
December 2005

Nepal	Ethiopia	Ghana	Uruguay	Nigeria	South Africa
3,466	3,410	2,520	2,428	2,412	2,010

The 10 states contributing the most uniformed UN peacekeepers were all low-income states, except for South Africa and Uruguay (upper-middle), and Jordan (lower-middle).

Countries	Years of existence as state	Number of international armed conflicts	State-based armed conflicts		
			Number of years in conflict	Number of battle-deaths on home soil	Number of conflicts
	1946–2005	1946–2005	1946–2005	1946–2005	2005
Afghanistan	60	2	28	562,628	1
Albania	60	2	3	38	0
Algeria	44	2	16	343,113	1
Angola	31	3	29	233,799	0
Argentina	60	2	9	4,215	0
Armenia	15	2	3	0	0
Australia	60	8	27	0	0
Austria	51	0	0	0	0
Azerbaijan	15	2	6	20,372	1
Bahrain	35	1	1	0	0
Bangladesh	34	1	19	53,500	0
Belarus	15	0	0	0	0
Belgium	60	5	7	0	0
Benin	46	0	0	0	0
Bhutan	57	0	0	0	0
Bolivia	60	0	3	1,682	0
Bosnia and Herzegovina	14	3	5	55,000	0
Botswana	40	1	1	0	0
Brazil	60	0	0	0	0
Bulgaria	60	1	2	0	0
Burkina Faso	46	1	2	150	0
Burundi	44	0	15	8,605	1
Cambodia	52	3	33	342,949	0
Cameroon	46	1	2	4,820	0
Canada	60	5	10	0	0
Central African Republic	46	1	2	219	0
Chad	46	7	39	43,921	1
Chile	60	0	1	2,095	0
China	60	6	24	1,309,146	0
Colombia	60	1	43	28,681	1
Comoros	31	0	2	83	0
Congo, Dem. Rep.	46	3	16	181,345	0
Congo, Rep.	46	1	6	9,791	0
Costa Rica	60	0	1	2,000	0
Côte d'Ivoire	46	0	3	1,200	0
Croatia	15	4	4	10,000	0
Cuba	60	3	19	5,307	0
Cyprus	46	1	1	6,311	0
Czech Republic	13**	4**	3**	0**	0
Denmark	60	5	6	0	0
Dominican Republic	60	1	2	3,276	0
Ecuador	60	1	1	39	0
Egypt, Arab Rep.	60	6	22	22,774	0

Non-state armed conflicts		Campaigns of one-sided violence	Score on Political Terror Scale	Number of refugees by country of origin	Number of Internally Displaced Persons (IDPs)	Use of child soldiers (under 18s) in active combat *	Regime type
Number of years in conflict	Number of conflicts						
2002–2005	2005	2005	2005	2005	2005	2001–2004	2005
2	0	1	5	1,908,052	176,596	Yes	Anocracy
0	0	0	2.5	12,702	0 or no data	No	Democracy
0	0	0	4	12,006	500,000	Inconclusive	Anocracy
0	0	0	3.5	215,777	61,700	Yes	Anocracy
0	0	0	2	856	0 or no data	No	Democracy
0	0	0	2	13,965	8,000	Inconclusive	Anocracy
0	0	0	1.5	44	0 or no data	Inconclusive	Democracy
0	0	0	1.5	66	0 or no data	Inconclusive	Democracy
0	0	0	3	233,675	558,387	Inconclusive	Autocracy
0	0	0	1.5	41	0 or no data	Inconclusive	Autocracy
0	0	0	4	7,294	500,000	Inconclusive	Democracy
0	0	0	2.5	8,857	0 or no data	Inconclusive	Autocracy
0	0	0	1.5	95	0 or no data	Inconclusive	Democracy
0	0	0	3	411	0 or no data	No	Democracy
0	0	0	1	106,537	0 or no data	No	Autocracy
0	0	0	2.5	269	0 or no data	Inconclusive	Democracy
0	0	0	2	109,930	183,400	No	Anocracy
0	0	0	2	4	0 or no data	Inconclusive	Democracy
1	0	1	4	370	0 or no data	Inconclusive	Democracy
0	0	0	2.5	4,254	0 or no data	No	Democracy
0	0	0	2	607	0 or no data	Inconclusive	Anocracy
2	0	1	4.5	438,663	117,000	Yes	Democracy
0	0	0	3	17,806	0 or no data	No	Anocracy
0	0	0	3.5	9,016	0 or no data	Inconclusive	Anocracy
0	0	0	1	122	0 or no data	Inconclusive	Democracy
0	0	0	3.5	42,890	212,000	Yes	Anocracy
0	0	0	3	48,400	200,000	Yes	Anocracy
0	0	0	1	938	0 or no data	Inconclusive	Democracy
0	0	0	4	144,228	0 or no data	Inconclusive	Autocracy
4	1	2	4.5	60,415	2,684,650	Yes	Democracy
0	0	0	1	61	0 or no data	Inconclusive	Democracy
3	0	2	4.5	430,625	1,664,000	Yes	Anocracy
0	0	0	2.5	24,413	123,500	Inconclusive	Anocracy
0	0	0	1	178	0 or no data	No	Democracy
3	2	0	4	18,303	500,000	Yes	Anocracy
0	0	0	2	119,148	4,900	No	Democracy
0	0	0	2.5	19,000	0 or no data	Inconclusive	Autocracy
0	0	0	2.5	5	265,000	Inconclusive	Democracy
0	0	0	2	3,589	0 or no data	No	Democracy
0	0	0	1	12	0 or no data	No	Democracy
0	0	0	3	67	0 or no data	Inconclusive	Democracy
1	0	0	3	770	0 or no data	Inconclusive	Democracy
0	0	2	3.5	6,291	0 or no data	Inconclusive	Anocracy

Countries	Years of existence as state	Number of international armed conflicts	State-based armed conflicts		
			Number of years in conflict	Number of battle-deaths on home soil	Number of conflicts
	1946–2005	1946–2005	1946–2005	1946–2005	2005
El Salvador	60	2	17	56,353	0
Equatorial Guinea	38	0	1	185	0
Eritrea	13	1	5	225,391	0
Estonia	15	3	2	667	0
Ethiopia	60	4	44	83,592	2
Fiji	36	0	0	0	0
Finland	60	0	0	0	0
France	60	19	24	1,180	0
Gabon	46	1	1	30	0
Gambia, The	41	1	1	650	0
Georgia	15	1	5	3,717	0
Germany	57	3***	5***	0***	0
Ghana	49	0	3	103	0
Greece	60	4	11	154,000	0
Guatemala	60	0	33	46,388	0
Guinea	48	1	5	1,400	0
Guinea-Bissau	32	1	2	9,005	0
Guyana	40	0	0	0	0
Haiti	60	0	3	419	0
Honduras	60	4	4	1,072	0
Hungary	60	2	2	3,171	0
India	59	4	48	83,130	5
Indonesia	60	2	41	63,585	1
Iran, Islamic Rep.	60	4	28	340,127	1
Iraq	60	5	41	462,133	1
Ireland	60	0	0	0	0
Israel	58	6	58	27,983	1
Italy	60	5	7	0	0
Jamaica	44	0	0	0	0
Japan	60	3	3	0	0
Jordan	60	5	9	4,222	0
Kazakhstan	15	1	2	0	0
Kenya	43	0	1	13,273	0
Korea, Dem. Rep.	58	2	16	627,418	0
Korea, Rep.	58	4	19	658,670	0
Kuwait	45	2	2	14,586	0
Kyrgyz Republic	15	1	2	0	0
Lao P.D.R.	52	3	19	24,005	0
Latvia	15	1	2	735	0
Lebanon	60	2	19	149,622	0
Lesotho	40	1	1	114	0
Liberia	60	0	12	12,684	0
Libya	55	4	25	4,250	0

Non-state armed conflicts		Campaigns of one-sided violence	Score on Political Terror Scale	Number of refugees by country of origin	Number of Internally Displaced Persons (IDPs)	Use of child soldiers (under 18s) in active combat *	Regime type
Number of years in conflict	Number of conflicts						
2002–2005	2005	2005	2005	2005	2005	2001–2004	2005
0	0	0	2.5	4,281	0 or no data	Inconclusive	Democracy
0	0	0	3	477	0 or no data	Inconclusive	Anocracy
0	0	0	3	143,594	50,509	Inconclusive	Autocracy
0	0	0	1.5	743	0 or no data	Inconclusive	Democracy
4	2	0	4	65,293	207,500	Inconclusive	Anocracy
0	0	0	1.5	1,379	0 or no data	Inconclusive	Democracy
0	0	0	1	5	0 or no data	No	Democracy
0	0	0	2	286	0 or no data	Inconclusive	Democracy
0	0	0	3	81	0 or no data	No	Anocracy
0	0	0	2	1,678	0 or no data	No	Anocracy
0	0	0	3	7,301	240,000	Inconclusive	Democracy
0	0	0	1.5	78	0 or no data	Inconclusive	Democracy
1	0	0	2	18,432	0 or no data	Inconclusive	Democracy
0	0	0	2	331	0 or no data	Inconclusive	Democracy
1	1	0	3.5	3,379	242,000	Inconclusive	Democracy
0	0	0	2.5	5,820	82,000	Yes	Anocracy
0	0	0	2.5	1,050	0 or no data	Inconclusive	Democracy
0	0	0	2.5	406	0 or no data	No	Democracy
0	0	1	4	13,542	0 or no data	Inconclusive	Anocracy
0	0	0	3	535	0 or no data	Inconclusive	Democracy
0	0	0	2	3,519	0 or no data	Inconclusive	Democracy
4	2	2	3.5	16,275	600,000	Inconclusive	Democracy
1	0	0	3.5	34,384	471,000	Yes	Democracy
0	0	0	3.5	98,772	0 or no data	Inconclusive	Autocracy
4	1	4	5	262,142	1,300,000	Yes	Anocracy
0	0	0	1	21	0 or no data	Inconclusive	Democracy
0	0	2	4	632	225,000	Inconclusive	Democracy
0	0	0	2	217	0 or no data	Inconclusive	Democracy
0	0	0	3	450	0 or no data	Inconclusive	Democracy
0	0	0	1	13	0 or no data	Inconclusive	Democracy
0	0	1	2.5	1,789	160,000	Inconclusive	Anocracy
0	0	0	2.5	4,316	0 or no data	Inconclusive	Autocracy
1	1	0	3.5	4,620	381,924	Inconclusive	Democracy
0	0	0	4	288	0 or no data	Inconclusive	Autocracy
0	0	0	1.5	268	0 or no data	Inconclusive	Democracy
0	0	0	2	381	0 or no data	No	Autocracy
0	0	0	2.5	3,122	0 or no data	Inconclusive	Anocracy
0	0	0	3	24,442	0 or no data	Inconclusive	Autocracy
0	0	0	2	2,430	0 or no data	No	Democracy
0	0	0	3	18,323	325,000	Inconclusive	Democracy
0	0	0	2	6	0 or no data	Inconclusive	Democracy
0	0	0	3	231,114	48,000	Yes	Anocracy
0	0	0	3	1,535	0 or no data	Inconclusive	Autocracy

Countries	Years of existence as state	Number of international armed conflicts	State-based armed conflicts		
			Number of years in conflict	Number of battle-deaths on home soil	Number of conflicts
	1946–2005	1946–2005	1946–2005	1946–2005	2005
Lithuania	15	2	3	8,620	0
Macedonia, F.Y.R.	15	1	3	145	0
Madagascar	46	0	1	7,080	0
Malawi	42	0	0	0	0
Malaysia	49	2	10	11,744	0
Mali	46	2	4	350	0
Mauritania	46	1	5	392	0
Mauritius	38	0	0	0	0
Mexico	60	0	2	144	0
Moldova	15	1	3	650	0
Mongolia	60	1	2	0	0
Morocco	50	3	18	16,514	0
Mozambique	31	1	16	139,749	0
Myanmar	58	2	57	72,573	3
Namibia	16	2	5	25,000	0
Nepal	60	0	13	11,021	1
Netherlands	60	8	15	0	0
New Zealand	60	5	23	0	0
Nicaragua	60	2	13	40,017	0
Niger	46	2	6	489	0
Nigeria	46	2	8	75,812	0
Norway	60	5	6	0	0
Oman	60	3	6	2,032	0
Pakistan	59	4	25	23,506	0
Panama	60	1	1	426	0
Papua New Guinea	31	0	7	323	0
Paraguay	60	0	3	4,250	0
Peru	60	1	21	31,046	0
Philippines	60	3	50	77,295	2
Poland	60	4	6	0	0
Portugal	60	8	18	0	0
Qatar	35	1	1	0	0
Romania	60	3	5	909	0
Russian Federation	60[††]	7[††]	33[††]	98,251[††]	1
Rwanda	44	2	12	9,759	0
Saudi Arabia	60	2	3	358	0
Senegal	46	3	12	1,644	0
Serbia and Montenegro	60[‡]	3[‡]	5[‡]	4,500[‡]	0
Sierra Leone	45	1	10	12,997	0
Singapore	41	0	0	0	0
Slovak Republic	13[**]	3[**]	2[**]	0[**]	0
Slovenia	15	0	0	63	0
Solomon Islands	28	0	0	0	0

Non-state armed conflicts		Campaigns of one-sided violence	Score on Political Terror Scale	Number of refugees by country of origin	Number of Internally Displaced Persons (IDPs)	Use of child soldiers (under 18s) in active combat *	Regime type
Number of years in conflict	Number of conflicts						
2002–2005	2005	2005	2005	2005	2005	2001–2004	2005
0	0	0	1	1,448	0 or no data	No	Democracy
0	0	0	2	8,599	770	No	Democracy
1	0	0	2	203	0 or no data	Inconclusive	Democracy
0	0	0	3	101	0 or no data	Inconclusive	Democracy
0	0	0	2.5	394	0 or no data	Inconclusive	Anocracy
0	0	0	2	520	0 or no data	No	Democracy
0	0	0	3	31,651	0 or no data	Inconclusive	Anocracy
0	0	0	—	27	0 or no data	No	Democracy
3	1	0	3	2,313	11,000	Inconclusive	Democracy
0	0	0	2.5	12,063	0 or no data	Inconclusive	Democracy
0	0	0	2.5	654	0 or no data	No	Democracy
0	0	0	3	93,572[+]	0 or no data	Inconclusive	Autocracy
0	0	0	3	104	0 or no data	Inconclusive	Democracy
2	1	1	4	164,864	540,000	Yes	Autocracy
0	0	0	2	1,226	0 or no data	No	Democracy
0	0	1	5	2,065	150,000	Inconclusive	Autocracy
0	0	0	1	159	0 or no data	Inconclusive	Democracy
0	0	0	1	4	0 or no data	Inconclusive	Democracy
0	0	0	2.5	1,463	0 or no data	No	Democracy
0	0	0	2	655	0 or no data	Inconclusive	Democracy
4	3	1	4	22,098	200,000	Inconclusive	Anocracy
0	0	0	1	15	0 or no data	No	Democracy
0	0	0	1.5	12	0 or no data	No	Autocracy
3	1	0	4	29,698	20,000	Inconclusive	Anocracy
0	0	0	1	42	0 or no data	Inconclusive	Democracy
0	0	0	3	23	0 or no data	Inconclusive	Democracy
0	0	0	2.5	44	0 or no data	Inconclusive	Democracy
0	0	0	2.5	4,865	60,000	Inconclusive	Democracy
0	0	0	4	465	60,000	Yes	Democracy
0	0	0	1.5	19,641	0 or no data	Inconclusive	Democracy
0	0	0	2	74	0 or no data	No	Democracy
0	0	0	1.5	11	0 or no data	No	Autocracy
0	0	0	2.5	11,492	0 or no data	Inconclusive	Democracy
0	0	0	4	102,965	265,000	Yes	Democracy
0	0	1	2.5	100,244	Yes[+++]	Yes	Anocracy
0	0	0	3	151	0 or no data	No	Autocracy
0	0	0	2	8,671	64,000	Inconclusive	Democracy
0	0	0	2.5	189,850	247,500	Inconclusive	Democracy
0	0	0	2.5	40,447	0 or no data	Inconclusive	Anocracy
0	0	0	2	39	0 or no data	Inconclusive	Anocracy
0	0	0	1	791	0 or no data	No	Democracy
0	0	0	1	155	0 or no data	Inconclusive	Democracy
0	0	0	1.5	27	0 or no data	Inconclusive	Democracy

Countries	Years of existence as state	Number of international armed conflicts	State-based armed conflicts		
			Number of years in conflict	Number of battle-deaths on home soil	Number of conflicts
	1946–2005	1946–2005	1946–2005	1946–2005	2005
Somalia	46	1	22	68,435	0
South Africa	60	3	28	3,775	0
Spain	60	7	11	245	0
Sri Lanka	58	0	22	62,044	1
Sudan	50	2	34	81,866	1
Swaziland	38	0	0	0	0
Sweden	60	0	0	0	0
Switzerland	60	0	0	0	0
Syrian Arab Rep.	60	4	22	19,972	0
Tajikistan	15	1	6	41,400	0
Tanzania	45	1	2	1,923	0
Thailand	60	6	31	6,200	1
Timor-Leste	4	0	0	33,525	0
Togo	46	0	2	55	0
Trinidad and Tobago	44	0	1	30	0
Tunisia	50	1	2	3,435	0
Turkey	60	5	27	36,299	2
Turkmenistan	15	0	0	0	0
Uganda	44	2	28	120,484	1
Ukraine	15	1	2	17,619	0
United Arab Emirates	35	1	1	0	0
United Kingdom	60	22	49	3,407	0
United States	60	17	32	189	1
Uruguay	60	0	1	53	0
Uzbekistan	15	2	4	107	0
Venezuela, R. B.	60	0	2	583	0
Vietnam	52††	5††	27††	2,488,532††	0
West Bank & Gaza	–	see Israel	see Israel	see Israel	see Israel
Yemen, Rep.	60†††	2†††	17†††	72,421†††	0
Zambia	42	0	0	0	0
Zimbabwe	41	2	18	27,000	0

Countries with a population under 500,000 are not included in this atlas, and neither are non-sovereign territories/dependencies, with the exception of the West Bank and Gaza.

* "Yes" means that the government and/or non-state groups used children in active combat. "Inconclusive" means unverified reports of children in active combat, or an unclear or under-18 recruitment age. "No" means that neither the government nor any non-state groups is suspected of using child soldiers.

** These data start in 1993, when the Czech Republic and the Slovak Republic were created. From 1946 to 1992, Czechoslovakia had one international conflict, one year in conflict, but no home-soil battle-deaths.

*** Pre-1990 data cover the Federal Republic of Germany (West Germany), created 1949, but not the German Democratic Republic (East Germany), a separate state from 1949 until it joined the Federal Republic in 1990. East Germany (1949–90) had no international conflicts, years in conflict or home-soil battle-deaths.

† This number includes 90,652 refugees from the Western Sahara.

†† As the Russian Federation is the successor state to the Soviet Union, pre-1991 data are for the Soviet Union as a whole. From 1991 to 2005, data cover Russia only.

Non-state armed conflicts		Campaigns of one-sided violence	Score on Political Terror Scale	Number of refugees by country of origin	Number of Internally Displaced Persons (IDPs)	Use of child soldiers (under 18s) in active combat *	Regime type
Number of years in conflict	Number of conflicts						
2002–2005	2005	2005	2005	2005	2005	2001–2004	2005
4	6	0	4	394,760	385,000	Yes	Anocracy
0	0	0	3	268	0 or no data	No	Democracy
0	0	0	2	49	0 or no data	Inconclusive	Democracy
2	1	0	4.5	108,059	341,175	Yes	Anocracy
4	2	3	5	693,267	5,355,000	Yes	Anocracy
0	0	0	2.5	13	0 or no data	No	Autocracy
0	0	0	1	75	0 or no data	No	Democracy
0	0	0	1.5	16	0 or no data	Inconclusive	Democracy
1	0	0	3	16,281	305,000	Inconclusive	Autocracy
0	0	0	3	54,753	0 or no data	Inconclusive	Anocracy
0	0	0	3	1,544	0 or no data	Inconclusive	Anocracy
0	0	1	4	424	0 or no data	Inconclusive	Democracy
0	0	0	2	251	0 or no data	No	Democracy
0	0	0	4.5	51,107	3,000	No	Anocracy
0	0	0	3	63	0 or no data	Inconclusive	Democracy
0	0	0	2.5	3,129	0 or no data	No	Anocracy
0	0	0	3.5	170,131	677,904	Inconclusive	Democracy
0	0	0	3	820	Yes†††	Inconclusive	Autocracy
2	0	1	4.5	34,170	1,740,498	Yes	Anocracy
0	0	0	2.5	84,213	0 or no data	Inconclusive	Democracy
0	0	0	2	30	0 or no data	Inconclusive	Autocracy
0	0	0	2.5	135	0 or no data	Inconclusive	Democracy
0	0	0	3	683	0 or no data	Yes	Democracy
0	0	0	1	111	0 or no data	No	Democracy
0	0	0	4	8,323	3,400	No	Autocracy
0	0	0	3	2,590	0 or no data	Inconclusive	Democracy
0	0	0	3	358,248	0 or no data	Inconclusive	Autocracy
see Israel	see Israel	see Israel	4	349,673	35,571	Yes	—
0	0	0	4	1,325	0 or no data	Inconclusive	Anocracy
0	0	0	3	151	0 or no data	Inconclusive	Anocracy
0	0	0	4	10,793	569,685	Inconclusive	Anocracy

††† Rwanda and Turkmenistan are known to have had IDPs in 2005, but there are no reliable numbers.

‡ As Serbia is the successor state to Yugoslavia, pre-1992 data are for Yugoslavia as a whole. From 1992 to 2005, data cover Serbia & Montenegro. In 2006, Serbia and Montenegro became separate states.

‡‡ From 1954 to 1975, Vietnam was two separate entities: Democratic Republic of Vietnam (North Vietnam) and Republic of Vietnam (South Vietnam). In 1976, North Vietnam defeated South Vietnam, forming the reunified Socialist Republic of Vietnam. Data for 1954–75 include both North and South Vietnam; in that period, South Vietnam had four international conflicts, 21 years in conflict and 1,130,298 home-soil battle-deaths.

††† In 1967, the former British-controlled territory of Aden became independent as the People's Republic of Yemen (South Yemen). In 1990, South Yemen merged with the Arab Republic of Yemen (North Yemen) to form today's Republic of Yemen. Data for 1946–67 cover only North Yemen. Data for 1967–90 include both South and North Yemen; in that period, South Yemen had two international conflicts, seven years in conflict and 12,296 home-soil battle-deaths.

Sources

The main data sources used:
Uppsala Conflict Data Program (UCDP), Uppsala University/Centre for the Study of Civil War, International Peace Research Institute, Oslo (PRIO) dataset, 2006.
Referred to as the UCDP/PRIO dataset, 2006.

Uppsala Conflict Data Program (UCDP), Uppsala University/Human Security Report Project (HSRP) dataset, 2006.
Referred to as the UCDP/HSRP dataset, 2006.

Bethany Lacina and Nils Petter Gleditsch, "Monitoring Trends in Global Combat: A New Dataset of Battle Deaths", *European Journal of Population*, 21, no. 2–3 (June 2005): 145–166. This dataset was updated and revised in 2006.
Referred to as the Lacina/Gleditsch dataset, 2006.

Centre for the Study of Civil War, International Peace Research Institute, Oslo (PRIO).
Referred to as PRIO, 2006.

Pages 6–7
THE WORLD BY REGION
Population data collated from The World Bank, Data & Statistics, Quick Query: World Development Indicators 2005 (accessed 26 September 2007).

1 When States Go to War
Page 10
NUMBER AND TYPE OF STATE-BASED ARMED CONFLICTS, 1946–2005
UCDP/PRIO dataset, 2006.

Page 11
REGIONAL DISTRIBUTION OF STATE-BASED CONFLICTS, 2005
UCDP/HSRP dataset, 2006.

REGIONAL TRENDS, 1946–2005
UCDP/PRIO dataset, 2006.

Pages 12–13
INTERNATIONAL ARMED CONFLICTS, 1946–2005
PRIO, 2006.

THE MOST WAR-PRONE STATES
The data are similar to that in a table in the *Human Security Report 2005*. However, the time-span and the coding rules differ slightly.

Pages 14–15
STATE-BASED CONFLICTS ON HOME SOIL, 1946–2005
UCDP/PRIO dataset, 2006.

Pages 16–17
TIME SPENT IN CONFLICT, 1946–2005
PRIO, 2006.

2 Warlords and Killing Fields
Data for all of the graphics in this section are from the UCDP/HSRP dataset, 2006. The Political Instability Task Force data on genocides and politicides discussed in the text is compiled by Barbara Harff.
See Barbara Harff, 'Genocide', www.humansecurityreport.info

3 Counting the Dead
Page 28
BATTLE-DEATHS IN STATE-BASED CONFLICTS, 1946–2005
Lacina/Gleditsch dataset, 2006.

Page 29
BATTLES-DEATHS IN NON-STATE CONFLICTS, 2002–2005
DEATHS FROM POLITICAL VIOLENCE, 2005
DEATHS FROM POLITICAL VIOLENCE IN EACH REGION, 2005
UCDP/HSRP dataset, 2006.

Pages 30–31
BATTLE-DEATHS IN STATE-BASED CONFLICTS, 1946–2005
Lacina/Gleditsch dataset, 2006 and UCDP/PRIO dataset, 2006.

THE MOST DEADLY CONFLICTS, 1946–2005
Lacina/Gleditsch dataset, 2006.

Pages 32–33
DEATHS FROM POLITICAL VIOLENCE, 2005
UCDP/HSRP dataset, 2006.

4 Measuring Human Rights Abuse
Page 36
DISPLACED PEOPLE, 2005
NUMBER OF REFUGEES AND IDPS WORLDWIDE, 1970–2005
Data from various sources collated by Phil Orchard, University of British Columbia, 2007.

Page 37
POLITICAL TERROR SCALE, 1980–2005
Linda Cornett and Mark Gibney, Department of Political Science, University of North Carolina Asheville. See http://www.unca.edu/politicalscience/images/colloquium/faculty-staff/gibney.html

Pages 38–39
HUMAN RIGHTS ABUSE
Political Terror Scale data from Linda Cornett and Mark Gibney, University of North Carolina Asheville, 2006.

Political violence death data from UCDP/HSRP dataset, 2006.

World Bank Political Stability and Absence of Violence Index, info.worldbank.org/governance/wgi2007, (accessed 16 March 2007).

Pages 40–41
CHILD SOLDIERS
Information on the use of child soldiers in combat from the Coalition to Stop the Use of Child Soldiers, Global Report 2004, www.child-soldiers.org/document_get.php?id=966 (accessed 9 July 2007).

Information on ratification of the Convention on the Rights of the Child, http://www.ohchr.org/english/countries/ratification/11.htm (accessed 28 September 2007).

Information on ratification of the Optional Protocol to the Convention on the Rights of the Child on the involvement of Children in Armed Conflict, http://www.ohchr.org/english/countries/ratification/11_b.htm (accessed 28 September 2007).

5 Causes of War, Causes of Peace
Page 44
STATE-BASED ARMED CONFLICTS AND UN PEACEKEEPING, 1946–2005
Armed conflict data from the UCDP/PRIO dataset, 2006.

Data on the number of peacekeeping missions from the United Nations Department of Peacekeeping Operations, www.un.org/depts/dpko/dpko/index.asp (accessed 25 January 2007).

THE RISE OF DEMOCRACY, 1946–2005
The Polity IV Project. See Monty G. Marshall and Jack Goldstone, "Global Report on Conflict, Governance and State Fragility 2007," *Foreign Policy Bulletin* (Winter 2007): 3–21.

Page 45
CONFLICTS BEGINNING AND ENDING, 1950–2005
UCDP/HSRP dataset, 2006.

Pages 46–47
WAR AND POVERTY
Data on World Bank Income Bands 2005, web.worldbank.org/wbsite/external/datastatistics0,,contentmdk:20420458~menupk:64133156~pagepk:64133150~pipk:64133175~thesitepk:239419,00.html (accessed 2 October 2006).

Conflict data from the UCDP/HSRP dataset, 2006.

Pages 48–49
CONFLICT AND REGIME TYPE, 2005
Data on regime type from the Polity IV Project.

Conflict data from the UCDP/HSRP dataset, 2006.

Pages 50–51
PEACEKEEPING AND ARMED CONFLICT
Battle-death data from the Lacina/Gleditsch dataset, 2006.

Data on UN peacekeeping operations from the United Nations Department of Peacekeeping Operations, www.un.org/depts/dpko/dpko (accessed 11 July 2007).

Data on the number of uniformed UN peacekeepers from the United Nations Department of Peacekeeping Operations, "Ranking of Military and Police Contributions to UN Operations, 31 December 2005", www.un.org/depts/dpko/dpko/contributors/2005/dec2005_2.pdf (accessed 17 July 2007)

Pages 52–59
DATA TABLE

Number of international armed conflicts and number of years in state-based armed conflict: PRIO, 2006.

Number of conflicts 2005: UCDP/HSRP dataset, 2006.

Battle-deaths: Lacina/Gleditsch dataset, 2006.

Number of years in non-state armed conflict and number of conflicts: UCDP/HSRP dataset, 2006.

Campaigns of one-sided violence: UCDP/HSRP dataset, 2006.

Political Terror Scale: Linda Cornett and Mark Gibney, University of North Carolina Asheville, 2006.

Refugees and IDPs: Various sources collated by Phil Orchard, University of British Columbia, 2007.

Child soldiers: Coalition to Stop the Use of Child Soldiers.

Regime type: Polity IV Project.

Index

Related Human Security Report Project Titles

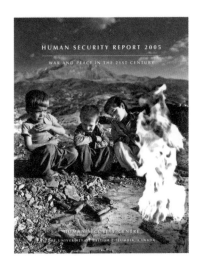

Human Security Report 2005

Documents a dramatic decline in the number of wars, genocides and human rights abuse over the past decade. Published by Oxford University Press, the *Report* argues that the single most compelling explanation for these changes is found in the unprecedented upsurge of international activism, spearheaded by the UN, which took place in the wake of the Cold War.

ISBN13: 9780195307399
ISBN10: 0195307399

Available in its entirety at www.humansecurityreport.info

To order, contact Oxford University Press or visit www.amazon.com

Human Security Brief 2006

Updates the *Human Security Report 2005's* conflict trend data and documents continuing declines in the number of genocides and other mass slaughters of civilians, and a drop in refugee numbers and military coups. Sub-Saharan Africa saw the greatest decrease in political violence in the period under review. Less encouraging was the finding that four of the world's six regions have experienced an increase in the number of conflicts since 2002.

Available in its entirety at www.humansecuritybrief.info

Notes on Terminology

Anocracy: *see* Democracy.

Armed conflict: political violence between two parties involving armed force, and causing at least 25 reported battle-deaths a year.

Armed group: any political group (other than a state) which employs armed force.

Autocracy: *see* Democracy

Battle-death: a death that is directly related to combat during an armed conflict. Can be a death of either a combatant or a civilian caught in crossfire. Does not include deaths from war-exacerbated disease.

Child soldier: individual aged under 18 in the armed forces of the state or of an armed group, whether or not the child is armed or is used in combat.

Civil war: an intra-state conflict causing at least 1,000 reported battle-deaths in a calendar year.

Civilian: an individual not in the armed forces of the state or of a non-state group; a non-combatant.

Combatant: an active and armed participant in an armed conflict, who may or may not be in uniform.

Conflict: in this atlas, always means an armed conflict. *See also* War.

Democracy, autocracy, anocracy: as used in the graph on p 44 and the map-spread on pp 48–49, a democracy is a state with well-established procedures for political participation, and with a freely elected chief executive who is subject to substantial checks and balances. An autocracy suppresses or sharply restricts political participation; selects its chief executive from within the political elite; and is governed with few or no legislative or judicial checks. An anocracy is neither fully democratic nor fully autocratic, and may be in transition from one to the other.

Displaced people: *see* Refugee.

Ethnic cleansing: the deliberate, organized and usually violent expulsion of people from an area because of their perceived ethnicity.

Extra-state conflict: an armed conflict involving a state which takes place outside its geographical borders. Most have been colonial wars.

Genocide: acts intended to destroy, in whole or in part, a national, racial or religious group: see pp 19–20. *See also* Politicide.

Home soil: a state or its territorial waters.

Human rights abuse: organized or sustained breach of human rights, such as torture or imprisonment without trial.

Income-band: the World Bank divides states into four groups by average income: see pp 46–47.

Internally displaced person (IDP): *See* Refugee.

International conflict: an armed conflict involving more than one state.

International war: an international conflict causing 1,000 or more reported battle-deaths in a calendar year.

Internationalized intra-state conflict: a conflict inside a state in which one or more outside states have sent their own armed forces to support one side or another.

Inter-state conflict: an armed conflict between two or more states.

Intra-state conflict: an armed conflict inside a state. *See* Civil war.

Militia: normally refers to the armed forces of insurgents, warlords, political parties or non-state groups. Also sometimes used for some armed forces associated with the state, usually those who are non-professional, part-time or raised during an emergency.

Non-state conflict: an armed conflict, usually between warlords or political, religious or ethnic groups, which does not actively involve the state. *See also* State-based conflict.

One-sided violence: organized and sustained attacks on defenseless civilians, by the state or by an armed group, causing at least 25 reported deaths in a calendar year.

Peacebuilding: measures designed to reduce tension or build confidence between opposing states or political, religious or ethnic groups, in order to prevent the start or resumption of armed conflict.

Peacekeeping: activities carried out primarily by foreign military personnel, usually under the mandate of the UN or a regional security organization, intended to maintain the peace in a post-conflict environment.